AdaptAbility™

Succeeding when Shift Happens in Work and Life

Dr. Wade A. McNair

with Lainie Cooney

Technics Publications

BASKING RIDGE, NEW JERSEY

Published by:

2 Lindsley Road
Basking Ridge, NJ 07920 USA
https://www.TechnicsPub.com

Cover design by Lorena Molinari
Graphics design by Sydney Sanchez
Edited by Sadie Hoberman

First Printing 2018
Copyright © 2018 by Wade A. McNair

ISBN, print ed.	9781634624374
ISBN, Kindle ed.	9781634624381
ISBN, ePub ed.	9781634624398
ISBN, PDF ed.	9781634624404

Library of Congress Control Number: 2018957105

Contents

CONTENTS

Acknowledgements

- To my family, for their unwavering support and always challenging me to be better today than yesterday, and better tomorrow than today. Thank you.

- To Lainie, my contributing author for her passion and commitment to creating workplaces that remain strong and successful in the midst of many shifts. Thank you.

- To Ron Smedley, my mentor and friend who has equipped, empowered, and encouraged me to live authentically, love unconditionally, and learn continuously. Thank you.

- To Sydney Sanchez, our Instructional Designer for her expertise in designing the graphics and the training tools for this edition. Thank you.

- To Dr. David Wilkinson at The Oxford Review for his commitment to academic excellence and providing ongoing research support for practitioners like myself.

ACKNOWLEDGEMENTS

- Finally, to Steve Hoberman, our publisher, for his guidance and support in our efforts to publish the book now in your hands. Thank you.

About the Author

Wade A. McNair, Psy.D.

Dr. McNair is a dynamic Coach, Consultant, and Communicator with over 20 years of experience in Talent Management, Corporate Learning, HR, Leadership, and Organization Development.

Wade is actively engaged in coaching and consulting with corporate, non-profit, and faith-based organizations. In addition to his professional practice, Wade is an Adjunct Professor at both the undergraduate and graduate levels. Wade has a Master's Degree in Organizational Leadership and a Doctorate of Psychology in Organizational Management and Change.

Wade's personal mission is to "live and help others live authentic lives where our actions and behaviors are in alignment with our assumptions and beliefs." He resides in Orange County, CA with his daughter Jordan, and their miniature schnauzer, Rory.

Lainie Cooney [Contributor]

Ms. Cooney is the Chief People Officer (CPO) of FanDuel Group, an innovative sports-tech entertainment company that is changing the way consumers engage with their favorite sports, teams, and leagues. FanDuel Group consists of a portfolio of leading brands across gaming, sports betting, daily fantasy sports, advance-deposit wagering, and television. In her role as Chief People Officer, Lainie leads the development and execution of the company's global people strategy.

Lainie brings over 25 years of experience designing and executing human resource strategies across geographically dispersed organizations, with deep expertise in HR technologies and systems, a focus on operational excellence, mergers and acquisitions, talent strategies and company culture and people engagement.

Lainie earned an MA in Clinical Psychology and Advanced Doctoral Studies at the California School of Professional Psychology. She is certified as a Senior Professional in Human Resources (SPHR) and a Six Sigma Black Belt.

About this Book

Life is made up of shifts - changes in our situations or circumstances. These shifts happen in our home life, our work life, and everywhere in between. As individuals, as teams, and as organizations, we experience almost daily shifts.

This book is designed to help us increase our Ability to not only survive, but thrive when these shifts happen. We move through the book using the ABC's of Development. First, we need to gain **Awareness** of the shifts we are going through, then we need to understand our **Behaviors** that result from these shifts, and finally we get the **Choice** on how to effectively navigate the many shifts we experience in our lives. By building our AdaptAbility, we will be better equipped to navigate the seemingly endless shifts in our lives.

The information contained in this book is not new. Thousands of hours have been spent researching the impacts that change has on our lives and how we can best adapt to these shifting situations and circumstances. The majority of this research already exists online or in journals or blogs about Change Management, Organizational Behavior, and Applied Psychology. Our goal in creating this book is to provide a tactical and practical tool to better equip others in managing personal and organizational change – based on best practices and solid empirical research.

As you explore the chapters, ask yourself the following questions: Who am I being? How does this information impact me in the real world? How can I apply what I am reading to the personal and organizational shifts I am experiencing?

All the best!

- W -

Understanding AdaptAbility

AdaptAbility Defined

Simply put, AdaptAbility is the ability to adjust to new conditions and situations. Every day, every person experiences changes that impact how we live our lives. Some changes we see as helping us, others we see as hindering us. As we grow and evolve, we realize that seeking AdaptAbility will engage, equip, and empower us to live better lives. Let's understand AdaptAbility in more detail.

First, AdaptAbility is an Ability. It is a competency or capability that can be developed, grown, and mastered. By understanding how we experience change, we gain confidence and feel better equipped to handle life when new conditions or situations arise. By also understanding how others experience change, we are able to improve our relationships and help our teams and organizations more effectively plan and manage change.

Second, AdaptAbility is a Choice. As humans, we are hardwired for connection. We are also hardwired to initially resist change, especially when that change is the result of someone else's choices. If we have insights into how we experience change, we can make better choices when shift happens.

In 1994, Desmond Tutu received the Nobel Prize for Peace for his role in the opposition to apartheid in South Africa. Amid national crisis and the dehumanization of his people, he said

> **"I cannot control what happens to me, but I can control how I respond to it."**

AdaptAbility is not only a skill we can develop, it is also a conscious choice we can make in response to the changes that occur in our lives and workplaces.

Third, AdaptAbility is a Journey. There is no magic spell or miracle pill that can make a person suddenly handle change effectively. AdaptAbility starts with a willingness to learn and a desire to grow in our own skills and abilities.

If we do not take the time to understand our own experiences with change, it makes it difficult to show understanding, respect, and compassion for others as they experience change. AdaptAbility requires experiences for us to learn from, to journey through, and form the foundation we need to build our skill and competence.

As you read through this book, ask yourself the questions on the following page.

These questions start your journey. And as you move through this book, you are encouraged to not just understand the concepts, but to move beyond the information and apply it to your real life.

Who am I being?

Am I building the skill of AdaptAbility?

Am I choosing to respond to life instead of reacting to happenstance?

Am I effectively managing change, or am I being managed by change in my life?

Underlying Principles and Assumptions

Before we go any further, we need to clarify some underlying principles and assumptions that underpin the ideas, insights, and information presented in the remainder of this book.

AdaptAbility and Change Management

Throughout this book the terms *AdaptAbility* and *Change Management* will be frequently used. They are not synonyms. As defined earlier, AdaptAbility is a competency or skill that can be developed. Change Management refers to the processes, practices, and tools used to manage the people side of change to achieve the desired (business) results.

> **Simply put, Change Management is a set of theories and tools that are used to build the competency and skill of AdaptAbility.**

In the book *RelateAbility*, the example of a QWERTY keyboard was used. We will use it again, but to describe the difference between AdaptAbility and Change Management. The example states that the keyboard is a fantastic invention and has many uses. However, if one does not learn to type, to build the competency or skill of using the tool, they will not be as effective as they could be. AdaptAbility is like typing, a skill that can be developed. Change Management is like the keyboard, a toolset we can learn to use to make our lives more effective at home and in the workplace.

Change has three primary causes.

Although change can happen in many different ways, there are only three primary causes of change in our lives.

- **Crisis** – Changes that are the result of crisis are immediately identified as having major impact on multiple areas of our lives, rather than limited to just one area. In most cases, a crisis-based change encompasses sub-changes that each will need to be worked through. For example, a divorce would be considered a change based on crisis as the impact of the change impacts finances, living location, parenting schedules, family relationships, and the personal impact of the termination of a critical relationship. Crisis-based changes are the most complex and often the most stressful of any type of change.

- **Chance** – Changes that are the result of chance are often seen as luck, fate, or random occurrences. For example, winning the lottery may have included the choice to purchase a ticket, but the change resulting from winning is purely based on chance. A forest fire that closes the freeway you use to get to and from work would also be seen as requiring change because of chance happenings.

- **Choice** – Changes that are the result of choice are the most common type of change we experience. Choice-based changes include choices we make for ourselves, like changing careers; or choices made by others, like being laid off from your job. Whether we are being impacted by others' choices or choices we make ourselves, it is important to understand how we experience change and how to manage it most effectively.

> When faced with new conditions or
> situations, it is helpful to be able to
> identify the primary cause of the change,
> not as a place of
> blame or accountability,
> but rather as a starting point to process
> the change in a purposeful way.

Change is neither "Good" nor "Bad".

If we look to the guiding systems in our body, we realize that the brain is our central command. Neuroscience has studied the brain and how our central command experiences change – be it from crisis, chance, or choice. Our brain's neuron network processes over two million bits of information every minute, yet we can only consciously hold five to nine thoughts at one time. This results in most of that information being unconsciously or subconsciously processed. As the brain's neuron network is made up of electrical impulses, they are not registered as good or bad. As such, our body's central command makes no differentiation or determination of whether change experience is good or bad for us, it is just information to be processed.

This is important for us to realize up front, because it gives us a better understanding why we will respond with the same levels of stress and emotions when dealing with a newborn baby not sleeping at night (which many would say is part of a "good" change) and the experience of losing a job and having to look for a new one (which many would say is part of a "bad" change). In a nutshell, change is what it is – a new condition or situation in which we can choose to either adapt or to resist.

Our experiences with change are predictable and sequential.

Research on personality and human behavior has shown that human beings are, for the most part, predictable in many of our behaviors.

Everyone needs to eat and sleep, we all have thoughts and feelings, and there are patterns in how we communicate and relate with others.

Research on change has shown that human beings experience change in ways that are predictable and sequential.

Not only do we go through six stages of change, each with a specific set of feelings, thoughts, and behaviors, but also that we go through these stages in a predictable order.

Understanding that people handle change similarly, but also sequentially, will help us be more aware and mindful of our own stages of change as well as better support others going through change experiences.

There are some characteristics of change that are unpredictable.

Although experiences with change are predictable and sequential, this does not mean that everyone will respond identically. There are some characteristics of experiencing change that are not as predictable and may even be considered unpredictable.

Although everyone will go through the six stages of change, how we respond in each stage will be different based on the value we place on the change and the impact that change has on our well-being.

Even though we will each experience predictable types of thoughts, feelings, and behaviors in each stage, the intensity and duration of each person's experience will be based upon the situation itself.

Some people will stay in a stage longer than others (duration) and some will experience the change with far more intensity. It is these characteristics, intensity and duration, that are most unpredictable.

So, one may ask, what basis do you make these assumptions about how people handle change?

Great question! The next section will go further in depth on the established psychological theory that we build our assumptions, beliefs, and competency development tools related to change management.

AdaptAbility and Established Psychological Theory

At the core of AdaptAbility is a model called the *Change Curve*. It is an applied model for better understanding the stages people go through when experiencing change. It is important that we understand the academic and scholarly research that has been conducted and that validates this model as we seek to build our AdaptAbility.

Change research has been conducted for decades. The earliest psychological model for change was introduced by Lewin in 1947 where he published a model that showed three stages of change – unfreezing, changing, and refreezing. In 1954, Maslow published his research known as the Hierarchy of Needs, providing insight to how people transition through predictable and sequential levels based on meeting specific motivational factors. McGregor's Theory X and Theory Y were published in 1960 and shed light on the importance of attitudes and cognitive framing of new situations based on personal mindset. This early research, however, did not provide a practical and tactical model that could be applied in the practice of managing personal and organizational change.

In 1969, the Change Curve was introduced as a model that had far reaching effects on our understanding of change and the ability to effectively manage change. The Change Curve was developed by Elisabeth Kubler-Ross in papers published in 1969 and 1970 in the "Journal of Psychiatry in Medicine". The initial model described the stages of grief and tracked the experiences we have in dealing with death and bereavement counseling, personal change, and trauma.

Between 1963 and 1971, Dr. Walter Menninger was conducting parallel research looking at how Peace Corps volunteers handled the change of being deployed to other countries. As a senior psychiatric consultant, he published the study in 1975 that presented a model that effectively mirrored Kubler-Ross' Change Curve.

In 1976, "Transitions: Understanding and Managing Personal Change" was published by three British Researchers. Adams, Hays and Hobson analyzed how people were affected by different types of change. Their research showed similar reactions, behaviors, and experiences to the Change Curve research by Dr. Kubler-Ross and the findings of Dr. Menniger.

In 1980, Dr. William Bridges published "Transitions: Making Sense of Life's Changes" and his research further supported the Change Curve. Additionally, his research went on to elaborate the methods of identifying which stage a person is experiencing and specific strategies for people in each stage to move forward most effectively.

In 1986, Dr. David Cooperrider of Case Western Reserve University published his doctoral dissertation entitled "Appreciative Inquiry: Toward a Methodology for Understanding and Enhancing Organizational Innovation." In his research, he argued that the scientific base of positive psychology offers organizations an understanding of human growth and change that challenges the prevailing view of people as 'resistant to change'.

In 1990, researchers Dottie Perlman and George Takacs conducted studies on personal reactions of nurses during organizational change in the healthcare industry. Their findings noted close alignment with the Change Curve and validated the application of Kubler-Ross' and Menniger's work to the organizational setting.

In 1990, Dr. Cooperrider published further details on the application of Appreciative Inquiry as it related to organizational change. In 1995, he published his "Introduction to Appreciative Inquiry" in the textbook *Organization Development (5th ed)*, making Appreciative Inquiry an established methodology for using positive psychology in the management of change.

In 1998, Schneider and Goldwasser furthered the research relating to leadership and change management. They published the modern graphic of the Change Curve that is most widely used in current Change Management toolkits and training.

In 1999, researchers Elrod and Tippett from the University of Alabama conducted a series of studies to validate the initial "performance dip" by teams experiencing change in organizations. Their empirical study of the relationship between team performance and team maturity was published in the Engineering Management Journal.

In 2002, Elrod and Tippet published a comprehensive study entitled "The Death Valley of Change" in the Journal of Organizational Change Management. Their research concluded that the Change Curve was scientifically valid. Additionally, they found that 13 of 15 previous studies had also found valid evidence for all the elements of the Change Curve.

In 2004, Dr. Clark reviewed the research conducted on the neuropsychology of decision-making and the performance dip experienced during the process known as "reversal learning" or "unlearning". Clark's research published in the Journal of Brain and Cognition reinforced the importance of reorientation, developing new skills, ways of working, and relearning when experiencing change-related performance dips. Also in 2004, Losada and Heaphy offered further evidence of the benefits of positive psychology and appreciative inquiry, and particularly positive

Change occurs on three levels and can be managed using the following three Points of View:

- **Micro** – This level refers to the level of individuals going through change. Here we will learn about how individuals think, feel, and how they behave when experiencing new conditions and situations. This is where we are able to better understand ourselves, and in doing so, better understand others. It is in this POV that we also realize that every team and every organization or community is really just the sum of the individuals within it. As such, we need to always keep this Micro point of view in mind as we seek to lead and manage change at any level. We will further explore this Point of View in Chapter 3: Personal AdaptAbility.

- **Mezo** – This level refers to the level of groups and teams. We will not dive into the individual definition of groups versus teams, other than to say that each are composed of two or more individuals working together. When these groups or teams experience change, they not only experience it as individuals (Micro POV) but also as a unit (Mezo POV). As we seek to lead and manage change, it is important that we understand how groups and teams experience development and change. We will further explore this Point of View in Chapter 4: Team AdaptAbility.

- **Macro** – This level refers to units consisting of smaller groups, organizations, and communities. In change management, this is often referred to as *Organizational Change*, although the practices used are not limited to just organizations. At this level, we must be aware that every Macro unit is made of groups/teams, and ultimately is the sum of the individuals that identify with that unit. There are specific practices unique to this level, but they must be integrated with the practices of the Micro/Individual and the Mezo/Team levels. We will further explore this Point of View in Chapter 5: Organizational AdaptAbility.

It is essential that we take into consideration each Point of View when implementing practices from the Change Management toolset.

For effective change to occur,
we must build AdaptAbility at each level:
individually,
groups and teams,
and organizationally.

Shift Happens!

Now to Next

The fundamental assumptions underlying any change in a human system are derived originally from research conducted by Kurt Lewin in 1947. For the last 70 years, the fields of psychology, sociology, anthropology, political science, economics, engineering, and even medicine have all been researching the impact that work has on people, and the impact that people have on the workplace.

Leveraging the best of many disciplines and research spanning the globe over decades, we come to what is recognized as the "nature of change". In the research we often hear terms like "interventions", "future state", "current state", "gap analysis", and "action planning". There are multiple Change Models, many with steps and sub steps. Some models are specific to a field or branch of science, like engineering or medicine. However, most of these change models reflect the same three phases that Lewin introduced in 1947.

I love what Dr. Edgar Schein, a leading expert in the fields of Organizational Culture and Change, said about Lewin:

> "I am struck once again by the depth of Lewin's insight and the seminal nature of his concepts and methods...[they] have deeply enriched our understanding of how change happens and what role change agents can and must play."

So, to keep things simple, and in honor of Lewin's original work, we have chosen to show the Nature of Change in 3 Phases: **NOW**, **TO**, and **NEXT**.

and our minds race to find some sense of stability and sanity.

Being in Stage 1 feels almost like driving in the fog, unable to clearly see the road ahead yet, and for your own safety, you must keep moving forward. Feeling almost nothing, we go on "auto-pilot" while trying to make sense of what we just heard or experienced. At this stage, our primary focus in on self-protection and a need to create a sense of personal safety and stability.

Stage 2: Doubt

Stage 2 brings our mind into the situation. We begin to assemble our thoughts about our circumstances and seek to gather more information. Doubt also triggers emotions like anger and frustration, causing resentment and blame to be our go-to behaviors.

When new information is presented, we will doubt the facts given and even doubt our own doubts. If we aren't careful we can get stuck in an "us versus them" pattern of thinking that creates a wall for any new, and often important information, to be heard and understood. At this stage, our primary focus is on being "right" and we have a need to gather facts and information to help process the shift we are experiencing.

Stage 3: Discomfort

Stage 3 creates a wave of emotional response. Anxiety, confusion, and feelings of being overwhelmed are common in this stage. This often progresses into a sense of depression or longing for how things used to be.

During this stage, there is a natural tendency to experience a lag or decrease in our performance and effectiveness. In this stage we may think that we are "off our game" or that we "really just don't care anymore" when asked about the change or shift we are experiencing. At this stage, our primary focus is on the problem to solve, and a need to reframe our perspective to consider the larger view of the situation or circumstance.

Stage 4: Decision

Stage 4 is all about making decisions and taking action. The first three stages had us "stuck in the past". Now we turn our face towards the sun and the bright future that this shift will bring with it. It is in this stage that we need to choose to take action, any action, that will move us forward.

Leveraging creativity, seeking ways to do things better, and embracing the opportunity to be an active participant in the change – these are the hallmark characteristics of this stage. It is in this stage that we welcome opposing views, we search for viable options, and have a renewed decisiveness. At this stage our primary focus is on finding solutions and a need to contribute to the path moving forward.

Stage 5: Discovery

Stage 5 is all about discovery and determination. We begin to grasp the meaning of the shift and enjoy a deeper understanding of the benefits and potential of this new way of being. We are energized, hopeful, and yet realize we haven't reached the finish line yet. In this stage we are challenged to finish strong and achieve what we have already determined to be our success in the situation or circumstance we find ourselves.

At this stage we are able to begin to realize the important insights and learning that have occurred in the process of our shift. We are in a heightened learning mode, seeking to build upon what we have learned about ourselves, about others, and about the very nature of change itself. At this stage our primary focus is on achievement and a need to fully integrate the insights we have gained.

 Stage 6: Development

Stage 6 is all about development and giving back. As the shift seems to become a memory and what was "new" now has become our "normal". We have reached the end of the Change Curve, yet feel there is still more we can do with what we have experienced. Here we realize we have fully transitioned from a survival mode to actually thriving beyond the situation or shift that began our journey through change.

When we can experience positive changes that result in our reaching this stage, we build resilience and adaptability for ourselves. AND, we realize that our experience has equipped us to help others as they transition through the same or similar shifts in their personal or work lives. We find the joy of being an advocate, support, mentor, or coach to others, allowing our insight and learning to be shared and leveraged in another person's change journey. At this stage our primary focus is on continuous improvement and a need to reach out to better others that need our help and support.

The Change Curve has become the empirical standard that we use to gain more awareness of how change impacts people, what they experience, and what they need, to successfully move from discomfort to discovery.

Many overlay the Nature of Change we referenced earlier with the Change Curve. Denial and Doubt would rest in the **NOW** box, Discomfort and Decision in the **TO** box, and Discovery and Development in the **NEXT** box. Although there is ample research to support an integrated view of the Nature of Change and the Change Curve, we find it less confusing if we keep them independent, while recognizing their interdependency.

Flipping a Coin

In many current books, presentations, and articles you will notice the statement that "70% of change efforts fail". This is an unsubstantiated claim and has no empirical research to support that statement. So, we must ask the question,

> **"What then is the overall success rate of change efforts?"**

Two separate studies, one from the consulting firm McKinsey & Company and the other from the consulting firm Prosci have placed the success/fail rate of change initiatives in organizations at an average 50/50 chance. Although not as high as 70%, if an investment is being made into an important change, be it in life or work, 50/50 chance just isn't good enough.

Unfortunately, when people choose a change – be it moving to a new city or adding a new software application to the organization – they choose it based on the expectation that it will be successful. Unfortunately, this "anticipated change curve" is a hope, not a reality. No matter how much we want to believe a change is beneficial, we must choose to plan effectively to manage the realities of how that change will impact ourselves and others.

We must start with Awareness. When humans experience change, we lose productivity and effectiveness. We call this the *performance gap*. When we fail to plan for this performance gap, we are effectively flipping a coin on whether the change will be somewhat successful or even a complete failure, such as implementing a technology that no one uses. However, when we realistically plan for impact of the change, we increase the odds of it being successful and minimize the intensity and duration of the performance gap.

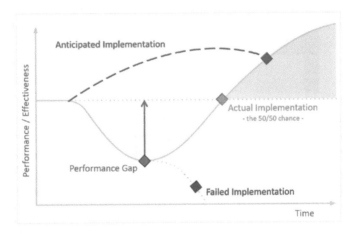

Most of what we have been talking about is referencing large scale or organizational change efforts.

How can we equip and empower effective change management at all levels – the individual, the group, the organization, and the community?

The answer is simple, change efforts fail when those making the change fail to address the needs of people at each stage as they go through change.

knowing that others may see the change differently than we do.

Often, we forget what it is like to *hear the news* because we have already moved through this stage. Whether individually, in a team, or as an organization, successfully moving through Stage 1 requires us to authentically acknowledge the fears and concerns that are being voiced. If we don't show care in how the news of change is initially received and how we respond, we will be set up for fighting harder and longer than is needed to help people through this stage. Additionally, it is important to be actively listening and willing to hear the initial emotional reaction with respect. Some may simply say "hmmm", while other will express far more emotive words or phrases. Ensuring alignment and safety means that questions will receive purposeful and timely responses.

 Success Strategy 2: Clearly Communicate

In the stage of Doubt, our primary focus is on communicating with clarity and consistency.

When leading a team or organization, it is important that messages be delivered consistently and at the same time and same way, to maximize alignment and reduce any additional confusion or fear.

The greatest hurdle to overcome in this stage is the tendency to assume the worst or fill in the information gaps with unreal data. As an organization, this is where the Frequently Asked Questions (FAQ) and Talking Points documentation is so vitally important.

I often get asked, "Do we just make up the questions for the FAQ and then answer them?" YES! You anticipate the types of questions that will be asked based on the circumstances of the shift and the impact to individuals and teams. By proactively answering questions, and filling in the information gaps with facts, we are able to best support people through this stage.

Let's be absolutely clear – clear communication is a leadership responsibility! I have experienced many cases of technology implementations where the change communication was left in the hands of a well-meaning IT project manager instead of the organizations' leadership, resulting in communication chaos and a very stressed out IT professional.

Communication MUST be:
Comprehensive and clear.
Purposeful and planned.
Responsibility and on the radar
of leaders at the top.

Obviously, the scope of the plan will depend on the scope of the project. However, having leadership support and alignment of messaging is critical to gaining the engagement needed to get through the next stage.

 Success Strategy 3: Create Engagement

In the stage of Discomfort, our focus needs to be on engaging the heart, mind, and hands of those going through this stage. Although there are exceptions to every rule, people want to have a good day, contribute positively to their lives, and make a difference.

I just don't believe that people wake up in the morning, get out of bed, and while stretching ask themselves, "How can I screw up today?" Humans are selfish creatures and we want to feel good about ourselves. Creating engagement requires understanding what motivates behavior and how to communicate in a way that excites the hearts and minds, and moves people into action.

In Chapter 6, we will discuss AdaptAbility and RelateAbility where we will review the Four Core Convictions that are shared by every person. These Core Convictions are the foundation for engagement. Our messaging should help others see how they will benefit from the change (Ambition), understand the value and importance of the shift (Belief), see how we are helping people through the change process (Compassion), and articulate an action plan with milestones and accountability (Discipline).

On a personal level, we will see others experience depression and lack of activity at this stage. To best support others on the individual level, we need to also engage them into action. It may be going to a movie, taking a walk, or beginning a new project. Often a physical or mental distraction can be the catalyst for us to shift from Discomfort to Discovery.

 Success Strategy 4: Build Confidence

In the stage of Decision, we have chosen to look forward instead of backwards. Seeking ways to reinforce the positive and build confidence are critical steps in this stage. I often refer to those experiencing this stage as *new drivers* – excited about the opportunity to drive, yet often scared to death of getting behind the wheel. Just as new drivers need practice driving under the guidance of an experienced driver, so do people need training, coaching, and support to feel confident and capable to really anchor the *new normal* during a time of shift.

We all have seen the TV shows where the parent yells at the new driver for missing the turn signal, only to realize that no one actually showed them where the lever was in the first place. Or the backseat driver is hassling the new driver to go faster and stop driving "like an old man". (Being an "old" man myself, I take that as a compliment to my safe driving habits.) We cannot rush someone into being confident, nor can we expect them to become capable without having the time and opportunity to learn.

Organizationally, this is where the value of the Training Plan becomes so vital to any change initiative. Knowing exactly what roles will be impacted, how they will be impacted, and the specific behaviors or skills needed in the **NEXT** stage should drive a comprehensive training plan to support employees in becoming *new drivers* when the situation or circumstances shift.

On the individual level, our role as coaches and friends is to encourage the movement forward, even if the steps are not as significant as we would like them to be. Think back to how parents respond when a child takes his/her first steps. They look awkward and tend to fall after a step or two. We don't sit them down and review the training plan on how to walk. Instead we encourage them and celebrate the steps they have taken. Unfortunately, when someone is going through a shift that has pushed them down, others are often quick to judge instead of cheering them on. Engagement has as much to do with others as it does with our own transition to Decision.

 Success Strategy 5: Share Knowledge

In the stage of Discovery, we have crossed over the hill and are picking up speed. We are excited, feel confident and are integrating the shift into lives. This is where we want everyone to be all along! In this stage, we need to celebrate the wins, acknowledge the challenge and look beyond the impact of the shift on us. In organizations, the leaders and early adopters reach this stage first. Remember, that until the entire organization or team is at Stage 5, there is still work that needs to be done.

Sharing experiences and storytelling are powerful tools in supporting those in other stages. We now have the opportunity to share our knowledge, our real-world experiences, our learning, and our journey through the Change Curve. A downside of this stage, however, is the tendency for us to forget there are others behind us needing support, or ignore the need to move forward into the final stage of change.

Highlighting success stories, honoring the service of our change champions, and giving credit for the hard work and progress are critical to maintaining the momentum of any team or organizational change. On the individual level, this is the time to take a moment and celebrate and express gratitude for what we have learned from the shift we have experienced. It is also an ideal time to thank friends and family that have been by our side throughout our shift and supported us through each stage of change.

 Success Strategy 6: Continuously Improve

In the stage of Development, we have reached the level of full integration. However, we can't assume that all is done. Is there a sustainment and maintenance plan in place? As the project team moves on, who has the responsibility to keep the system running or to continue the improvements needed to optimize the process? These are critical questions to ask. If not addressed, shift may be only temporary or become a *book of the month* initiative that leaves not lasting and not impactful. Having a post-change plan is critically important to making the change really "stick" in the team or organization. Change fatigue is a real issue that can arise if too many changes are introduced in a short timeframe.

Think about team and organizational changes like remodeling a vintage car. The project may come to completion as we show off the shiny new vehicle to our friends and neighbors, but without ongoing maintenance it will become ineffective and break down. The purpose of the restoration was not just to launch the new look, but to have a viable source of transportation.

> Change resistance is a real issue that can arise if changes are completed but show no benefit for the energy and effort it took to implement them.

On the individual level, we all know about our New Year's Resolutions. We make changes and, if we follow through with them, we see good results. However, if we don't have a plan to sustain or reinforce the new behaviors, we will revert back to our old habits. As change champion and coach, we need to realize that the celebration of reaching a milestone is an awesome moment to reach. We also need to recognize the need for ongoing support and care, especially if those we are supporting are working through shifts that have life-long impact.

So, what happens if we fail to meet the needs of a stage as we are managing a shift?

The image below is an adaption of a graphic shared by T. Knoster at a conference in 1991. In this adapted version, we see each of the success strategies needed to support people though each stage of change. We can also see the logical result of that change if one of the strategies is missing or incomplete.

CHAPTER 3

Personal AdaptAbility

Feelings, Thoughts, and Behaviors

Earlier in this book, we reference the Change Curve and the importance of this model to navigating change in our lives. As we look specifically at the Micro or Individual level of change, we can further explore each of the six stages and the feelings, thoughts, and behaviors that we can expect from ourselves and others.

As a reminder, the experience we have in each stage is sequential and predictable. Each of us will go through each stage beginning with Denial and hopefully successfully passing through Discomfort to Discovery, and ultimately into a place of Development and continuous improvement.

At each stage we will experience similar feelings, thoughts, and behaviors. However, we will differ in the intensity and duration of our responses. Individual differences in values, priorities, personality, stress, support systems, and other factors will change how long we spend in each stage (duration) and how powerful each stage is expressed (intensity).

We should never judge people for not moving faster or for expressing themselves in a way that would be different than ourselves. Each person is unique and, although there is a predictability of how we all go through change, we will each experience the same change in different ways.

**Always seek to understand
and build trust with those going through
major shifts, even if we may not
experience the same shift
in the same way.**

---

to make shift, our thoughts are cynical and skeptical, and our overall behaviors are resistant and obstinate.

In this stage we often think to ourselves that the shift makes no sense and that there is no way that this change could be in your best interest. Often, we refer to the change as happening **TO** us and look for anyone or anything we can blame in the situation.

To most effectively transition through to Stage 3, we need create engagement for ourselves and others. To most effectively transition to Stage 4, our greatest ally is information. It is okay to hold a position or ideal, if we are willing to listen and evaluate additional information.

In this stage, we often lose sight of the big picture and need to ask good questions to gain an accurate picture of the situation. Being proactive, respectful, and using our intense feelings to be probing and insistent on getting the facts will help resolve our questions and doubts. Ultimately, to transition into Stage 3, we need to reframe the shift to one we can logically understand, even if we don't agree with it.

 Stage 3: Discomfort

The third stage in the Change Curve is Discomfort. Reaching stage 3, we begin to feel the weight of the shift we are experiencing. We have come to terms that the change is happening, and even understand the change, but feel overwhelmed, anxious, frustrated, and even uncaring about the situation.

We struggle with being non-participative and unorganized, often feeling we are going around in circles and not accomplishing anything. Our overall behaviors are unproductive and inconsistent.

In this stage we often are frustrated and want to give up. We think that anything else would be better than the situation we are going through. We let thoughts like "who cares?", "this is hopeless", or "this will never work." dominate our mind and cause us further confusion.

To most effectively transition through to Stage 4, we need to take action. This may be mental action like creating a gratitude list of what you are thankful for in the shift, or creating a list of the pros and cons of the change. It is important that we focus on the future state of the situation rather than commiserate in what we are leaving behind.

This stage is, in my opinion, the most critical in moving from a *just survive* mindset to one of *even thrive* mindset. The choice is one of action – doing something that will help move you forward – mentally, emotionally, even physically. I have been involved in changes where the only thing I could do was take a walk to clear my mind and reconnect to what I could do in the moment to move myself forward.

We are holistic beings, meaning that everything in our lives impacts everything else in our lives. As such, taking time for fun, or exercise, or organizing in other areas of our lives will have a positive impact on the change we are experiencing. Positive and purposeful distractions can have a ripple effect and re-engage our hearts, minds and hearts – better preparing us for re-engaging the change and transitioning to the next stage on the Change Curve.

Ultimately, the gap between Stage 3, Discomfort, and Stage 4, Decision, is the direction we are facing. If we are focused on the past, on what was and a refusal to let go, we will get stuck in Discomfort. In fact, we may begin a cycle that revisits Denial and Doubt. I call this cycle the *Wallow Waltz*. Denial, Doubt, Discomfort... Denial, Doubt, Discomfort... (imagine Waltz music playing as you read those three words aloud).

However, we have a choice. If we choose to look forward, to what could be, to what may be, to the positive impacts of the shift, we propel ourselves into the next stage and exit the trap of the *Wallow Waltz*. By focusing on the **NEXT**, we cross the hurdle and begin to thrive in the shift rather than just survive it.

 **Stage 4: Decision**

The fourth stage in the Change Curve is Decision. If getting out of Stage 3 is all about

Action, then moving through Stage 4 is about making empowering decisions. Having just moved beyond the past and focused on the future, we are excited and anticipating what lays ahead on our journey. Our thoughts are creative and ideas are free-flowing. We have energy and yet, so many options to choose from!

In this stage we often find ourselves being indecisive, puzzled, confused, and contradicting ourselves. We see other points of view so much clearer and are ready to take the next steps. We have options to consider and are anxious to make moves that will maximize the success of the change we are experiencing.

To most effectively transition through to Stage 5, we need to be open to the ideas of others. Using a method like *Rational Decision Making* will help guide our decisions to take into consideration facts and data over the excitement we will be feeling at this stage.

As we move through Stage 4 and into Stage 5, we need to practice perspective. Keeping in mind that, although we are heading full speed into Discovery, there are others that are still working through the earlier stages of the Change Curve and will need our encouragement and support.

 Stage 5: Discovery

The fifth stage in the Change Curve is Discovery. Reaching this stage is a reason to celebrate! It is here that we understand the change in such a way that we acknowledge the benefits and desire the successful completion of the change.

In this stage we often wonder why others are complaining or dragging their feet. Don't they understand how this shift is better than the status quo? We have effectively embraced the change, possibly at the risk of becoming insensitive and impatient with those that have not.

This stage seems to me like when we get the cold or flu. When we are going through the discomfort of a runny nose, sore throat, body aches, coughing, and fever, we believe our lives are ending! We curl up on the sofa with a blanket, and if we are lucky, someone else makes us soup and puts on our favorite movie so we can fully rest. After time off work, and feeling well again, we return to our normal routine. However, if someone we know "falls ill", we tend to dismiss their discomfort and tell them to "suck it up" and "push through". Once we have moved into Discovery, we often forget how it felt to be in denial, doubt, and discomfort.

To most effectively transition through to the final stage of Development, we need to acknowledge that progress is being made and encourage those that are still on their way to Discovery. It is in Discovery that we need to celebrate the quick wins, maintain momentum, be approachable, patient, and never forget to give credit to those that have earned it.

Finishing strong is a mindset that we need to challenge ourselves to maintain. We don't want to fizzle out only a few feet from the finish line!

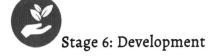 **Stage 6: Development**

The sixth stage and final stage in the Change Curve is Development. Here we realize the full impact of the shift. What was **NEXT** becomes the **NEW NOW**. There is a feeling of satisfaction and a desire to focus on maximizing the **NEW NOW** to gain the full benefits of the shift we have experienced. It is in this stage that we transition from experiencing the change, to ideally, becoming a mentor, coach, or leader to others that are still within the Change Curve.

In this stage we may risk becoming seen as pretentious or even arrogant in that we "know it all", we have "been there, done that", and have "moved on" from that project or initiative. This is a recipe for failure.

Every shift requires further fine-tuning, maintenance, and ongoing development. It is here that we enter into the practice of continuous improvement.

It is similar to having purchased a new piece of furniture from IKEA. Let's make it a desk. You have cleared out the old space and evaluated what you will keep and what will be discarded or recycled. You have taken the time and energy to unpack all the pieces, and with some effort, successfully built your shiny new desk. It looks perfect!

However, if you don't maintain the desk by dusting or keeping your workspace organized, your desk could possibly become an eyesore or, even a place where all other things in the house go to rest. To fully experience the benefits of having the new desk, we must focus on keeping it maintained and sustain its functionality as a desk (versus a laundry pile).

From Discomfort to Discovery

As mentioned earlier, I believe the most critical point of the Change Curve is the gap between Discomfort and Discovery. Between them we find the Stage of Decision.

It bears enough importance to summarize what we shared earlier about this critical point in the Change Curve:

Avoid the Wallow Waltz:
Denial, Doubt Discomfort (repeat).
If we choose to look forward,
to what could be, to what may be,
to the positive impacts of the shift,
we propel ourselves to the next stage:
DISCOVERY!

By focusing on the **NEXT**, we cross the hurdle and begin to thrive in the shift rather than just survive it.

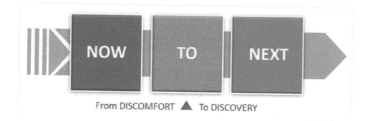

From DISCOMFORT ▲ To DISCOVERY

Let's take a moment to discuss the idea of Fear – a significant component, and primary cause of, the *Wallow Waltz*. There are three types of fear we need to be aware of:

- **Future-based Fears** are based on not knowing what the future holds. A core desire of humans is stability, and any shift

in our lives can cause us to fear the
unknown. We like things to stay the same.
We get comfortable in what we know. We
get into patterns of behavior that give us
confidence. We buy brands that make us
feel content. When shift happens, we then
experience the stages of the Change Curve.
Sometimes something as simple as our
preferred deodorant being discontinued
can launch us into denial, doubt, and
discomfort.

- **Past-based Fears** are based on attributing a
current shift or change with the experiences
of a past shift or change, often with
negative impact. Studies have been
conducted on the impact of psychological
scarring on the abilities to effectively adapt
to new shifts or changes in our lives. For
example, if you were forced to move on a
regular basis as a child, and those moves
resulted in the loss of friendships and
feelings of being alienated and alone, the
opportunity to move your family to a new
location to accept a promotion may trigger
fears that seem irrational to others, but are

real for you because of experiences in the past.

- **Identify-based Fears** are based on how we see ourselves, our worth, and our value. So often we compare ourselves with others, change our behaviors because of others' expectations, and give up on our passions and giftedness because we feel they are insignificant or irrelevant. These behaviors are based on a fear that you aren't enough... good enough, strong enough, pretty enough, thin enough, wealthy enough, or so many other lies that we have been led to believe.

Be encouraged! You are a unique individual and you have value and worth because you draw breath!

You have immeasurable greatness, gifts and talents, choices and potential to fully experience all that is already within you. If you don't believe me, ask those that love you and support you – for your identity and self are not to be feared, but to be celebrated and embraced!

In opposition to these fears, we can instead embrace the three following strengths as we seek to move from Discomfort to Discovery:

- **Curiosity** – The value of wonder is often undervalued in our change efforts. We experience fear and assume that it is real. We perceive a situation and immediately make judgement on what is and is not happening. Often, we find that, when presented with new data, we were incorrect in our interpretation. The phrase "I wonder..." has such far reaching impacts. It places us in a position to receive rather than reflect. It brings us to a place of willingness to understand instead of just being understood. And it moves us beyond our own viewpoint to see a bigger and more wonder-full experience.

- **Courage** – Research by Dr. Brene Brown on shame and guilt shows that the single difference between those that experience love and belonging (group A) and those that do not experience love and belonging (group B), is that those in group A have a BELIEF that they are WORTHY of love and belonging. They have the courage to see beyond their fears (be they future, past, or identity) and choose instead to dare greatly. If this paragraph "hits you hard", then I encourage you to Google Brene Brown and view her TED Talks. Personally, she has played a transformational role in my life, specifically in the area of identity-based fears.

- **Compassion** – Being wrong is being human. In each of our memories there is a moment we remember making a massive mistake. We blew it. We missed the mark. Unfortunately, when we experience failure, we often trigger fear. In fact, some of you had a small panic attack when that failure came to mind! We remember how others handled the situation, what we felt about ourselves, and the impact our error had on others.

> **It is in these moments that we must choose to show ourselves compassion. Not a single person on this Earth is perfect.**

And although it is a wonderful ideal to pursue, the shame and guilt of not measuring up to our own expectations is often disheartening. In showing ourselves compassion, we also unlock another strength - when we show compassion to ourselves, we increase our ability to show compassion to others! If we are to be leaders of change, having compassion for others will be a critical strength as we support others through the Change Curve.

Moving from Discomfort to Discovery is ultimately a choice. Will we be curious and seek to find the best in what the shift can offer? Will we have the courage to embrace the new opportunities or seek safety in the status quo? Will we face the reality that change isn't always fun, and choose to show compassion to ourselves and others as we experience the challenges of change.

While researching for this chapter, I saw the following saying and found it to be quite fitting:

To **FEAR** is to:
Forget Everything And Run
or Face Everything And RISE
either way, it is your **CHOICE**.

Transitioning from Discomfort to Discovery is making a choice to break through instead of shutting down. At the beginning of this book I referred to the ABC's of Development. As we build **Awareness** and understand the **Behaviors** associated with building AdaptAbility at the individual level, it is ultimately up to us to **Choose** how we will respond when shift happens.

Become a Change Champion

Having completed the Change Curve, we can embrace the opportunity to give back to those that have not yet reached Discovery. It is when we reach the conclusion of the Change Curve that we have another choice to make. Will we simply move on, or will we give back? If we have survived cancer, will we volunteer to mentor the newly diagnosed patient? If we have overcome adversity and addiction, will we reach out and support those that continue to struggle with their own?

Again, we discuss the ABC's of Development. Having reached this final stage, we are now Aware of the toll that shifts have on our well-being. Having reached this final stage, we understand the Behaviors and how we can best support and influence moving through the Change Curve. Having reached this final stage, we also have a Choice. Will we choose to simply move on, or will we choose to use our experience to make a difference in the lives of others?

This is our ultimate choice, and an opportunity to become someone's Change Champion! You don't need a degree or formal education to qualify for this role. You don't need to have years of experience on your resume to be effective. To be a Change Champion, you need to first want to be a Change Champion.

With that accomplished, the best *Shift Leaders* demonstrate the following behaviors:

Ability to build relationships
(RelateAbility)

Desire to represent the needs and
interests of others

Seeks to understand others before having
to be understood

Clarity and transparency in their
communication

Willingness to learn new things and
embrace new ideas

Effective in planning and following
through on commitments made

Passionate about making a difference,
always for the better

Whether the shift is being experienced by an individual, team, or organization, we need Change Champions! They advocate for others best interest, communicate an empowering vision, help provide oversight and insight to those experiencing the change, and help drive focus and accountability to experience successful shifts.

Team AdaptAbility

From Storming to Performing

Although there are numerous definitions of groups, and their differences between teams, work groups, family structures, associations, and other multi-people systems, we will be using the widest possible definition in this chapter.

We will not dive into the individual definition of groups versus teams, other than to say that each are composed of two or more individuals working together. When these groups or teams experience change, they not only experience it as individuals (micro point of view) but also as a unit (mezo point of view).

As we seek to lead and manage change, it is important that we understand how the group/team level experiences development and change.

The Tuckman Model (below) represents the sequential and predictable path a group/team will take in their development. It is widely researched and referenced when working to create and build effective teams in organizations. It has also been successful in working through group challenges as they deal with change as it mirrors the Change Curve.

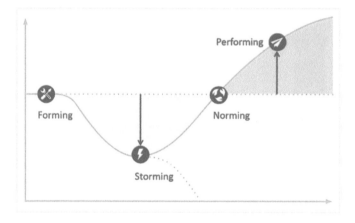

Let's look at Tuckman's model and the parallels it has with how people experience change individually.

Similar to the Change Curve, where we reviewed the thoughts, behaviors, and feelings experienced at each stage, Tuckman identified three experiences that teams will go through as they move through his development model. They are:

- **Content** – what a team does, their work, and their performance results

- **Process** – how a team works together and steps they take to achieve their goals

- **Feelings** – the relational dynamics of the team and how members interact with each other

Tuckman's research suggests that most teams concentrate almost exclusively on content, to the detriment of process and feelings, which explains why teams which are strong in theory often lack the effectiveness they desire.

Stage 1: Forming

The first stage of group and team development is Forming. In this stage, team members are introduced and establish initial working relationships. Processes are often formal and general information is shared between members (job title, years at company, and experience). Communication is professional and personal information is kept to a minimum.

- **Content** – In this stage, individuals attempt to define the job to be done. They seek to accomplish *first steps* to experience accomplishment in some way.

- **Process** – In this stage, team members will seek insight and guidance from leaders and project sponsors. They are just beginning the process, and having best practices to guide them will increase their time to Performing and minimize the performance dip experienced in Storming.

- **Feelings** – In this stage, team members are experiencing feelings similar to the first two stages of the Change Curve including shock, confusion, and anxiety, and are looking for safety and guidance in how best to relate with the new team. Team Development training, like RelateAbility, provides new skill building in Emotional Intelligence and better equips and empowers team members to successfully navigate from Storming to Performing.

Many groups do not move beyond the Forming stage. We call these groups Working Groups, as they are working together in some way but have little or no interdependence with each other's work. A working group can be an effective staffing strategy, especially when individuals are being associated with a group label or location.

 Stage 2: Storming

The second stage of group and team development is Storming. Just like the name infers, this is not the most pleasant stage of team or group development. Egos and emotions play a big role and the balance of power is being established. As personalities clash, priorities differ, and communication skills are tested, Storming will take some time, resources, and care to effectively resolve into Norming.

- **Content** – In this stage, team members seek to control actions that most align with their best interests. Actions are debated and members will resist any demands made upon them that don't match with their desired way of doing things.

- **Process** – In this stage, processes are often non-existent. If there are processes established by an organizational team development guide, team members will push back and look for reasons not to do it "their way". Often a mindset of *whoever controls the process, controls the team* will be seen at this stage, with members vying for power and control.

- **Feelings** – In this stage, people are anxious and uncomfortable. Emotions and egos are being hurt, often without intent. Unable to effectively communicate or relate with others creates further hurdles for team members to overcome. RelateAbility training in the Forming stage has shown to greatly reduce the frustration and anger often experienced in this stage of team and group development. By better understanding ourselves and others, and being given tools to better communicate and resolve conflict, organizations can see a decrease in the performance gap experienced at this stage as well as an increase in the speed to which the team reaches the Norming stage.

It should be noted that some teams and groups never leave this stage. They settle into ineffective ways of working, often adversarial and sometimes even toxic. Although they may refer to themselves as a team, they are really just teams caught in conflict and we refer to them as Pseudo-Teams. They may pretend to be working well together, but the reality of their experience is hard-fought, awkward, and stressful.

Stage 3: Norming

The third stage of group and team development is Norming. In this stage, the team reaches agreement on their mission, vision, values, and goals. They begin to process the necessary action steps and implement procedures and project plans to help keep everyone on track and timely in their roles and responsibilities. Here the team fully understands the interdependence needed by every member to fulfill the objectives the team is tasked to achieve.

- **Content** – In this stage, there is open exchange of ideas about the matters at hand. This is the phase where "working meetings" are most frequent as there is much to discuss and debate. Later in this Norming stage, team meetings become *update* or *status* meetings to keep the team aligned and on task.

- **Process** – In this stage, the team establishes their Team Charter, SMART Goals, Decision

Matrix, and other formal policies and procedures. These are documented and form the foundation for how the team will address upcoming issues, problems, decision, and resource allocation.

- **Feelings** – In this stage, team members see each other as interconnected and begin to have a more open and accepting view of team member differences. Trust and respect of each other is building in this stage and patterns of behavior are beginning to feel "normal" when working together. It is important to note that Norming does not require team members to all be friends or socialize outside of the workplace. Many teams successfully norm and perform while maintaining only professional relationships. However, these professional relationships do require a level of trust, understanding, and openness in order to be effective.

Many teams are "effective enough" at the Norming stage that they don't pursue further development. Short-term project teams or event-based teams that seek to effectively norm and reach time-bound objectives find this stage to be an effective base of operations. Like people development, some are content and happy to be individual contributors and not manage other people. This does not negate them as employees, but rather provides insight as to how they are motivated and experience their work life. In this case, pushing someone to become a people manager when they have no desire to do so, would be unwise. Similarly, if a team is effective in its basic functions, placing formal pressure to further develop may not be in the team's best interest.

 Stage 4: Performing

The fourth stage of group and team development is Performing. This is the easiest stage to observe, but the most difficult to attain. Performing requires the team to be working like a well-oiled machine. Roles and responsibilities are clear, there is a high level of trust and accountability, and performance is meeting and often exceeding expectations.

- **Content** – In this stage, actions are consistent and the team has a reputation for achievement and follow-through.

- **Process** – In this stage, the team seems to have mastered the process of decision-making, prioritization, planning, and delivering on expectations. It is important to note that performing teams will sometimes need to return to Norming if there are changes in timelines, deliverable expectations, or resource allocation.

- **Feelings** – In this stage, the team is more an experience of a family than of a work team. Individually there is trust between members and there is a group trust in the team competence and capability to meet expectations. Communication is now more informal and the team leverages the different viewpoints and the diversity of membership. It is important to note that, depending on the make up of the group, having members leave or new members join will reduce effectiveness as the team re-Norms. There is even the possibility that the team will re-enter the Storming phase if the balance of power on the team is impacted. For example, a larger percentage of the team membership is changed, either purposefully or ad-hoc.

Some teams will further develop and seem to have the *magic* or *synergy* to consistently operate beyond expectations. These teams are rare, but they are incredibly effective and the holy grail of team development. When a person has been on one of these *magic* teams, they are forever changed. We refer to these ideal teams as having reached the stage of High-Performing.

 Stage 5: Adjourning

The final stage of group and team development is Adjourning. This stage was added years after Tuckman published his original work on team and group development. As project teams began to trend, there was a need to further extend the model to include the process needed for Psychological Closure.

Whether it be an individual team member leaving the team to pursue an important initiative, or the entire team reaching the completion of a year-long team project, this is a moment of change. It is here that the Change Curve begins again, with team members experiencing a sense of loss and, again in need of Psychological Safety.

There are ways to plan for this Adjourning stage of team and group development. For instance, celebrating victories and accomplishments, showing gratitude to those that helped make the effort better, and giving credit where credit is due. When people have a positive experience on a project team, we don't want their last experience to be one of loss, doubt, and discomfort. If the last team experience is not managed, team members may not be willing to participate in another team initiative. Planning for Psychological Closure also promotes the positive experience for those looking in from the outside and those wanting to continue working on team projects.

Tuckman highlighted a number of important observations from his research on teams and teamwork which still have resonance today:

A team will not be fully effective unless it reaches the stage of performing/ interdependence.

Many teams will not get beyond Forming and be effective Working Groups.

Some teams accept Storming as a normal way of operating, which I refer to as Toxic Teams.

Unless the team transitions fully into Norming they may revert back to Storming.

Like the Change Curve, the amount of time (duration) and intensity that each team takes to transition from one stage to another will vary depending on the team composition. Composition will ultimately determine how quickly a team will transition from Storming to Performing. These factors include its size, location of team members, the length and frequency of meetings, how the team members relate with one another, stability of team membership, external influences, and the natural pressures that occur with deadlines and prioritization of goals and objectives.

Managing Team Change

Richard Hackman of Harvard University conducted research and discovered that less than 10% of team members agreed on who were members of their team! This hinders AdaptAbility.

Not having clarity in why the team exists, what the team is expected to accomplish, or even who is on the team are hallmarks of a team or group in crisis. If team members can't agree on who they need to work with, what they are to do, or how they will validate success, there is little chance the team will reach the Norming Stage, let alone the Performing Stage of development.

As such, we will focus on these three areas in helping teams manage the changes they experience.

For a group or team to have any chance of success, they must have the following 3M's:

- **Mission.** Every member must be aware of what success looks like to the team and why it's important. Having a clear sense of urgency for why the team was created and answering "why now?" is critical to the clear understanding of the team mission. Additionally, every member should be able to articulate the priorities and how each priority contributes to the success of the larger team missing an initiative. If members don't understand the bigger picture then they're limited in their judgment. With impaired judgment comes poor decision-making.

- **Membership.** Effective and performing teams exceed expectations because they set the conditions and proactively define their work for optimal performance. They're clear on roles, responsibilities, and expectations of each person, and they hold members accountable for their actions. Strong teams believe that producing results is the price of membership.

- **Metrics.** Part of being accountable and responsible is knowing what each member is accountable and responsible for. Metrics outline the expectations of the team results and should clearly align with the priorities set forth in the mission. Metrics should be the logical conclusion for decision making authority and articulate what success looks like. As such, everyone will be on the same page and working towards the results and timeline.

For a team to manage change effectively, they need to be the right solution for the right problem. If they lack Mission, Membership, and Metrics, they will not adapt and become irrelevant, regardless of their formal title or power of the participants.

Building Team Effectiveness

What makes a great team also contributes to effective change teams (those leading a change). In 2016, Google released their findings from a multi-year research project on team effectiveness. The project was called "Project Aristotle" based on the quote: "the whole is greater than the sum of its parts" as the Google researchers believed employees can do more working together than alone.

I encourage any research junkies to take a look at the project in detail – global participants, double-blind interviews, testing on team composition (personality, skills, demographics), testing on team dynamics (emotional intelligence, development processes), almost 200 teams, and over 250 correlated items from their longitudinal engagement study on work and life – then using over 35 different statistical models on hundreds of variables, they sought to identify factors that:

- Impacted multiple outcome metrics, both qualitative and quantitative

> **If I make a mistake on my team,
> it is not held against me.**

If you strongly agree with this statement, then you are experiencing a high level of Psychological Safety. If you strongly disagree with this statement, then there are concerns that need to be addressed in how safe it is to risk new ideas or make mistakes with your team.

Dependability

Credibility and dependability are closely related. Credibility is *doing what you said you would do*, whereas dependability refers to the *consistency of your behavior*. Dependability is determined when team members can rely on the quality of work you provide. Both dependability and credibility are essential to building and maintaining trust. Research has shown that the largest determining factor on whether a team is effective in meeting their goals has to do with trust – trust that there is Psychological Safety and trust that the team members are Dependable and can be counted on to meet their commitments.

To assist in evaluating whether a team member has Dependability, Google created this test statement:

> **When my teammates say they'll do something, they follow through with it.**

If you strongly agree with this statement, then you are experiencing a high level of Dependability. If you strongly disagree with this statement, then there are concerns that need to be addressed around trust, credibility, and the consistency of team members fulfilling their responsibilities to the team.

Structure and Clarity

People often leave jobs because they lack a real understanding of what is expected of them, and how their job responsibilities impact the overall mission of the organization. This is the same for teams. Clear roles and responsibilities, job expectations, expected processes to be followed, and the consequences of performance are important to team effectiveness.

Goals can be set at the individual or group level, and must be **SMART** (**S**pecific, **M**easurable, **A**ctionable, **R**elevant, and **T**imebound). Also, critical for this component is a clear decision-making process. One of my favorite decision making acronyms is **RAPID**. It stands for **R**ecommend, **A**gree, **P**erform, **I**nput, and **D**ecide.

For each decision, determine what letter is assigned to those involved. This also helps create clarity for those who think they have Decision authority, but really are only being involved to have their support or recommendation.

Without Structures and Clarity in place, teams cannot fully reach the Norming phase of development. Much of the Storming phase is coming to alignment and agreement on the structure, roles, responsibilities, and expectations. Additionally, having clear understanding and readily available information around expectations are critical for moving through Stage 2 (Doubt) in the Change Curve. Without this component, team members are left confused and anxious, or worse, confidently incorrect in their understanding.

To assist in evaluating whether a team member has Structure and Clarity, Google created this test statement:

Our team has an effective decision-making process.

If you strongly agree with this statement, then you are experiencing a high level of Structure and Clarity. If you strongly disagree with this statement, then there are concerns that need to be addressed on the expectations, roles, responsibilities, mission, vision, and performance of each member, and the team as a whole.

Meaning

Every person wants their work to have meaning, to invest their time and efforts into something that makes a difference. Gallup conducted research on employee engagement, and they found the single most influential factor in employee engagement was if people had made relationship connections, or *a best friend at work.*

Finding meaning doesn't have to connect to just the product, it could also connect with the people you work with. As I have mentioned before, humans are hardwired for connection. We each desire to belong, to be valued, and to be part of a *tribe.* We spend over half our waking hours in the workplace – often more time with our co-worker *tribe* than our family *tribe.*

Having meaning individually, and as a member of a team is critical to team effectiveness and working through change as a team. Finding a sense of purpose can be found in the relationships, the work itself, or the output of the work. Regardless of where meaning is found, it is important to realize that our actions impact others. When we move from Discomfort to Discovery, or from Storming to Norming, we are often not doing this alone.

To assist in evaluating whether a team member has Meaning, Google created this test statement:

The work I do for our team is meaningful to me.

If you strongly agree with this statement, then you are experiencing a high level of meaning and connection with your team. If you strongly disagree with this statement, then there are concerns that need to be addressed relating to team purpose, communication, trust, relationships between team members, and team identity.

Impact

All work is evaluated. All teams are evaluated. This should not be a surprise to anyone. The results attained by the team create a sense of accomplishment, especially when those impacts are of high priority and value. When individuals on a team are unclear on that impact, or the team itself has confusion on how they contribute to the greater good, effectiveness is negatively impacted.

To help build Impact means understanding how your role and function directly or indirectly align with and support the Mission, Vision, and Values of the organization. For example, if an organization has a Value on Customer Service, then every person's role should have a direct or indirect impact on the customer experience. Similarly, a team should be able to connect their team mission, vision, and performance goals with enabling the organization to better perform and reach organizational goals.

To assist in evaluating whether a team has Impact, Google created this test statement:

I understand how our team's work contributes to the organization's goals.

If you strongly agree with this statement, then you are experiencing a high level of impact as a member of the team and/or as a team together. If you strongly disagree with this statement, then there are concerns that need to be addressed relating to your team's understanding of its purpose, mission, vision, and the value they bring to the organization.

Whether you are looking to be a change agent within a team, or be a team that leads change, understanding both the Change Curve and the Team Development Curve will form a foundation for successful teaming. By further understanding and applying the team effectiveness tools mentioned in this chapter, you increase your odds of becoming an ideal team member and being a part of a truly effective and highly performing team.

Organizational AdaptAbility

The Individual Mandate

Every organization is simply the sum of its parts. In organizational change, people make up the most critical component. For an organization to reach its first major milestone in a change initiative, the majority of people impacted by the change must have successfully transitioned from Discomfort to Discovery. Unfortunately, once individuals have reached Discovery, they often forget what it was like to go through Denial, Doubt, and Discomfort. In organizational change, doing so has a disastrous effect.

As the graphic on the facing page shows, there is a cadence of Discovery that needs to happen before the organization can effectively reach the "new normal" or **NEXT**.

According to research, organizations fail to reach their change goals due to the following:

- Managers not understanding the fundamental principles of change management

- Managers falling to the temptation for *quick fixes* or *simple solutions*

- Managers not fully appreciating the significance of the leadership or cultural responsibilities of change

- Managers not appreciating the significance of people and their experience of change

- Managers lacking the credibility and trust of those they lead

will not necessarily hold much urgency in a change that only benefits the stockholders of the company (unless they own stock).

> **At the heart of any change messaging, we must clearly articulate the "why" and the "why now", and do so for all levels of the organization.**

Step 2: Form a Powerful Coalition

Many organizations miss the opportunity to develop a powerful change leadership team. The benefit of taking the time to purposefully and practically consider the best members to be in change leadership cannot be overstated.

Involving different functions, levels, and types of employees (part-time, full-time, individual contributors, supervisors, etc.) provides the best opportunity to understand how the change will affect their peers and those they influence. The tendency is to create teams of people we already know will support the change often leaving out those with high influence, those highly impacted by the change, or those with the potential to derail the initiative.

If we can successfully build a team of diverse voices, perspectives, and experiences, we are better equipped to navigate organizational change.

Step 3: Create a Vision for Change

Many change initiators feel that it is their responsibility to craft the vision and mission that should be communicated to the organization. This is not supported by research. In fact, the best people to craft this message are the guiding coalition that has been selected to lead this change. Leveraging the information gathered in Step 1, the change leadership team, with consult of the executives and change initiators, should craft the larger communication plan.

Realizing that many on the change leadership team may not have marketing and communications experience, it is vital that these internal or external resources be provided to the change leadership team. It should also be noted that these marketing communication professionals should not have the authority to demand or direct, but rather coach and consult.

Most organizations attempting to manage change neglect to prioritize Steps 2 and 3, resulting in a less effective or even failed change initiative.

 Step 4: Communicate the Vision

An email isn't a communication plan. An effective change management communication plan will leverage every possible means of communication to create a strong, singular, and successful change message. Using visual communication like display boards, posters, and intranet sites provides mass messaging that can be seen by many. Voicemail broadcast, vlogs, and announcements in team meetings, provides the human connection needed by most people experiencing the Change Curve.

It is said that only 7% of a message is understood when sent via text or email. Adding tone of voice and the human connection increases that understanding to 45% of the message. Providing context and interaction further expand the understand ability of the message being sent.

**In a nutshell,
face to face is best,
voice to voice is effective, and
email communication
should be only a supporting action.**

Step 5: Empower Action

Successful changes involve the head, the heart, and the hands of everyone being impacted by the shift. When power is held tightly at the top or quietly communicated in meetings of the elite, resistance will build. The more people involved, the better the chances of success.

Empowerment will begin with the initial communication of the vision by the change leadership team – if that team effectively represents a wide breadth of the organization.

Empowering action involves delegation. Delegating is effectively entrusting others with the power and responsibility to do or enact a part of the mission and vision. Notice the word "entrust." Leadership trust is the single most powerful resource that an organization has in leading and managing change. We demonstrate this trust by involving others and delegating.

Empowering action also involves demolition. Removing obstacles and providing a clear path for those with change responsibilities is just as critical as delegating.

> When management *steps up to the plate* and makes empowering decisions, they reduce conflict and further build trust.

Step 6: Create Quick Wins

Quick wins don't just happen! They require a plan that is systematic, purposeful, and practical. Real change takes time and any change risks losing momentum if milestones and moments are not celebrated. However, it is impossible to celebrate something that hasn't been measured or been part of a plan to achieve.

> Without short term wins,
> those that were once supportive
> of the change can lose heart
> and join the ranks of the naysayers
> and those that are resisting the shift.

A good rule of thumb is to hold monthly or quarterly celebrations that highlight progress and show appreciation to those that have contributed to the progress. Additionally, taking time to individually acknowledge those that have gone above and beyond will further build trust and goodwill.

Step 7: Build on the Change

Be careful not to declare "mission accomplished" when there is still work to be done! There will be a temptation to declare a change complete when the first major milestone is reached. Doing so will result in decreased morale and the possibility of losing momentum completely.

Balancing phases and stages with metrics and milestones that are planned well in advance and consistently communicated, will reduce the temptation to declare victory prematurely.

As we reinforce and refresh troops on the battlefield, we also need to reinforce and refresh those leading change. In long-term change initiatives, having a staffing plan that provides terms of service (like a senator or member of congress) can provide team members with the option to continue with the project while opening opportunities for others to join.

This is also a great time to revisit and reinforce the "why" and "why now" messages that can get lost with the passage of time.

Step 8: Make It Stick

Culture is defined as "the way we do things around here." Until a change has been anchored into the culture, it is not considered successful. Earlier, I shared the incorrect assumption that "70% of change efforts fail." Although there isn't empirical evidence to support that claim, it is understandable as so many change efforts never succeed in becoming culture.

Integrating the expected behaviors into onboarding, orientation, professional development, and other forms of organizational learning and development is essential to anchoring the change. Having a maintenance and sustainment plan that is agreed to prior to the change completion will significantly contribute to the success of your change initiative.

It is imperative that leaders recognize (and take full responsibility), for guiding and modeling the behaviors they desire and expect of others as they lead their change initiatives.

Kotter's research provides practical and tactical actions we can take to reduce change failure. By integrating his research with the Nature of Change and the Change Curve, we build a robust toolkit and further develop our AdaptAbility.

AdaptAbility and Culture

A research survey conducted by the Katzenbach Center had similar conclusions as other change research in that only about half of organizational change projects accomplish and sustain their goals. What was interesting about the Katzenbach research is the focus they had on culture as it relates to transitions and transformation initiatives in organizations. The data from the participants showed:

- 84% think culture is critical to business success

- 60% say culture is more important than strategy or operating model

- 45% do not feel their culture is being effectively managed

- 47% do not feel culture is not a priority for their leadership team

- 24% said their company used existing culture to drive the change effort

that we are not able to cover in this book. However, it is important to recognize that culture will either be effectively guided and nurtured, or will evolve on its own.

Culture can either be our greatest opportunity in organizational change, or it can be our biggest obstacle.

CHAPTER 6

AdaptAbility and RelateAbility

Better Together

Understanding how people communicate and are motivated is as important as understanding how they experience each stage of change. It really isn't a question of which you need more, but rather the integration of both skillsets to maximize our effectiveness.

So often, change efforts fail because there is a lack of trust and low levels of RelateAbility when teams interact with each other. By building AdaptAbility and RelateAbility skillsets together, we can be far more effective in managing the people side of change – be it in our own lives or in our workplaces.

In short, RelateAbility is the *ability to effectively relate to others*. RelateAbility also includes the potential for transformational relationships with each person we interact with, personally and professionally. In academic terms, we also refer to RelateAbility as *Emotional Intelligence*.

RelateAbility uses the TeamRelate Model as a tool to help build our competency and skill. The TeamRelate Model has two primary components: Communication Styles and Core Convictions.

AdaptAbility and Communication Styles

Understanding Communication Styles

Communication Style is a description of an individual's natural preference of focus and function. Every individual has components of all

Communication Styles, but it is the strongest or most natural style that dominates the rest.

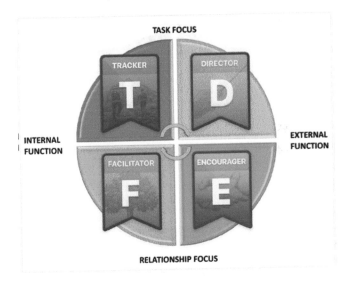

For quick reference, below is a summary of the four Communication Styles:

- **Director (D):** The Director style refers to the degree to which an individual needs to be in charge or in control. They are highly task-focused and prefer to interact with and lead others.

- **Encourager (E):** The Encourager style refers to the degree to which someone is externally and socially-oriented. They are highly relationship-focused and prefer to interact with and influence others.

- **Facilitator (F):** The Facilitator style refers to the degree to which an individual is purposeful and patient. They are highly relationship-focused and prefer to work in small groups or collaborate behind the scenes.

- **Tracker (T):** The Tracker style refers to the degree to which an individual is careful about "tracking down" and taking care of details. They are highly task-focused and prefer to work in small groups and lead processes.

Communication Styles and Change

When working with people, we want to communicate in a way that builds connection. Below is a quick summary of how each Communication Style interacts, specifically what they say, what they hear, and what they need in the practice of change management. Remember that in change, they will demonstrate these behaviors at different levels of intensity and duration depending on the importance and impact that change has in their personal viewpoint.

Directors (D) need to be in charge and in control. They are strong-willed, and they expect their ideas and decisions to prevail and to be respected.

- *What they say:* Only what is seen as relevant, brief, and bottom line

- *What they hear:* Sometimes only what they want, and will tune out if too much detail is given

- *What they need:* For you to get to the point, be factual, and less emotional

Encouragers (E) are highly sociable, people-oriented, outgoing individuals, who are good communicators with a persuasive Communication Style. They are good at encouraging and motivating others.

- *What they say:* They say a lot, often exaggerate to make a point, and speak with emotion

- *What they hear:* Broad strokes of conversations, often missing details. They tend to interrupt

- *What they need:* They need you to let them talk and share their emotional enthusiasm

Facilitators (F) tend to be a calming force who prefer supportive roles. They are nice people to have around because they seek understanding in situations and work hard to gain approval. Facilitators pride themselves on being part of the team, as well as their role in facilitating team effectiveness.

- *What they say:* They don't say much and tend to be reserved and speak in friendly, gentle tones, often asking questions for better understanding

- *What they hear:* Everything. When others won't listen, Facilitators will

- *What they need:* They need to be appreciated for listening

Trackers (T) prefer to follow-up and carry out assignments given to them by authorities they respect rather than to initiate action steps conceived on their own.

- *What they say:* Everything in detail. They give you the whole story
- *What they hear:* Everything, but want more. Need detail or can feel misled
- *What they need:* More than anything, they need to be understood. Listen to them, and ask for clarity

AdaptAbility and Core Convictions

Understanding Core Convictions

The four TeamRelate Core Convictions are based upon the following two Dimensions:

Intrapersonal/Intrapersonal and Preservation/ Promotion.

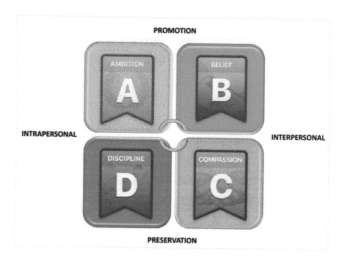

Each individual has their own core values and set of beliefs. To try and create a framework that takes into consideration every value and every belief of every person would be foolish. Instead, TeamRelate looks at four Core Convictions that have the greatest impact on RelateAbility. They are (A) Ambition, (B) Belief, (C) Compassion, and (D) Discipline.

For quick reference, below is a summary of the four Core Convictions:

- **Ambition:** Ambition refers to the degree to which an individual is *forward-looking* and proactive in achieving significant goals.

- **Belief:** Belief refers to the degree to which an individual trusts in and lives according to a predefined system of truth.

- **Compassion:** Compassion refers to the degree to which an individual feels compelled to help others.

- **Discipline:** Discipline refers to the degree to which an individual is able to sustain focus and dedication toward the completion of a task or goal.

Core Convictions and Change

When working with people, we want to communicate in a way that promotes engagement. As opposed to Communication Styles, Core Convictions change over time, and their development has a significant impact on an organization and an individual's capacity to work within certain environments. Understanding how each Core Conviction contributes to organizational success, should help in developing the sense of urgency and align motivations that are essential to the change management process. Here is a brief overview of each Core Conviction and the impact they have on individual and team engagement.

- **Ambition (A):** If Ambition is the strongest conviction, these individuals are proactive in reaching goals—an achiever. The conviction of Ambition provides an organization with energy to complete projects and inspire teams. Establishing a sense of urgency and tapping into the future vision is where the conviction of Ambition can be leveraged, especially in times of change and uncertainty.

- **Belief (B):** If Belief is the strongest conviction, these individuals value integrity, fairness, and moral excellence. The conviction of Belief can provide an ethical perspective when difficult decisions need to be made. Decisions in change management have consequences, and those with Belief as a core conviction help promote the organizational values and culture, especially in times of change and uncertainty.

- **Compassion (C):** If Compassion is the strongest conviction, these individuals possess a rare quality for giving to others in need. The conviction of Compassion provides an organization with a client-centered perspective. Those with Compassion as a core conviction provide a much-needed balance to the change process, as their focus will be on the impact of the change on people, not just on profits.

- **Discipline (D):** If Discipline is the strongest conviction, individuals have the ability to sustain their focus and dedicate themselves to the completion of a task or goal. The conviction of Discipline provides an organization with tenacity, helping them *stay the course* and never lose sight of their stated objective and goal. When many change efforts fail because they lack process or lose their sense of urgency, those with Discipline as their core conviction will be essential to keeping the project on task, in scope, and within budget.

Having diversity of Core Convictions in your change leadership will help provide insight for the project as well as assist in understanding the needed messaging and change management practices that will best motivate every individual involved in the change initiative.

For more information about RelateAbility, Communication Styles, and Core Convictions, please read the book, "RelateAbility: Working Together To Make Work Life Better" by Wade McNair and Ted Malley.

CHAPTER 7

AdaptAbility and Workforce Engagement

AdaptAbility in a Multi-Cultural World

Earlier we talked about the importance of culture in effectively managing Organizational Change. Let's take a few moments to expand beyond the specific culture of the organization, to research on the dimensions of culture globally.

Hofstede's Culture Dimensions are a powerful tool in building both our AdaptAbility and our RelateAbility. By being able to better understand a person's culture, we can better build relationships with them. And the same cultural dimensions that are experienced by people around the world are also experienced in teams and organizations. As such, if we have a tool that helps us better define our culture – be it individually, as a team, or as an organization – we can better reinforce, support, and sustain the culture we have, or further develop our cultures as we desire.

It is important to note that there is a *right answer* with this tool. Each aspect of culture is valued and valid as a reality for people around the world. Although we may share patriotism for our country of birth, it does not negate the culture and identities of others that have a culture different than our own. This tool is to help build awareness and understanding of the incredible cultural diversity we share in our communities and workplaces.

Hofstede identified six cultural dimensions in his research. Each dimension is a continuum with seemingly opposing ideals on each end of the dimension, and individual cultures will fall somewhere between them. Please be wary of the temptation to assume that descriptors on the right are more positive and the left are negative. There are no values-set for the dimensions, they are just

It is imperative that when talking about culture at any level – the individual, the group or team, and organizationally – we must first be willing to listen and understand another perspective before requiring our own perspective to be understood.

On a side note: As an Organizational Psychologist, there is one terminology change I would make if this were the "McNair Cultural Dimensions". I would reframe the Masculinity/Femininity dimension as a Task/Relationship Dimension.

Gender norms around the world are evolving and there is overwhelming evidence of gender being irrelevant to both the preference for achievement, heroism, assertiveness, and materials rewards, and the preference for cooperation, modesty, compassion, and quality of life. As such, looking at this Dimension as Task and Relationship removes the gender bias and focuses on the specific behaviors and preferences instead.

AdaptAbility and Continuous Organizational Change

The Change Curve ends at Stage 6 (Development). In this stage, we focus on continuous improvement and anchoring the change into the organizational culture. But what happens after that? If every change ever made is in a state of continuous improvement, then wouldn't that mean the organization is in a constant state of change? The simple answer is YES.

David Garvin of Harvard University addresses this question in his research. He contends that continuous improvement requires a commitment to organizational learning. Organizations that have this commitment to ongoing learning as part of their culture are called Learning Organizations. Research shows that Learning Organizations are healthier places to work because they:

- Encourage independent thought and reasoning
- Increase ability to manage change (AdaptAbility)

Once there is clarity in vision and mission, alignment of culture with the goals of continuous change, and leadership that has built credibility and trust, it is now necessary to have practices and policies in place that will reinforce the desired behaviors.

When creating these reinforcing processes, people want to be engaged and equipped, not cattle prodded and criticized. Knowing the behaviors desired and placing positive reinforcement when achieved, is the surest way to build engagement around continuous learning culture.

Similar to needing to align the walk with the talk, supporting leaders need to make a commitment to being measured on the results. If there is no purposeful plan, dedicated resources, and actions being taken, the initiative to build a culture of continuous learning will eventually fall by the wayside. People move when they are being measured. Leadership prioritizes performance metrics, especially when linked to pay.

Overall, to create a Learning Organization and a culture of continuous improvement, there must be voice and action at the top of the organization to support the change.

Culture of Continuous Improvement

One of the primary forces in building a culture of continuous improvement is Psychological Safety. This is a term that I wish more organizations and leaders were actively aware of. In short, experimenting or learning new things naturally causes anxiety.

Psychological Safety is having a culture where employees are encouraged to experiment and stretch themselves in their development. This means that the pain and discomfort of unlearning or relearning will be possible, worthwhile, and supported.

In addition to Psychological Safety, a culture of continuous improvement requires the following four characteristics: Appreciation of Differences, Openness to New Ideas, Allocation of Time and Resources to Learning, and Communication of Progress. The story of the Sticky Note by 3M is a great example of how these factors enabled an initial experiment to become the largest revenue generating product for the organization.

Defined Learning Structure

There needs to be a defined learning structure in place to support the continuous learning culture. A Learning Organization will make sure to have formal processes, tools, and training to equip and empower new learning and improvement.

As such, there will need to be, at a minimum, a path for Experimentation, a process for Information Collection, a means to Analyze the Information, and a method of Measurement to determine if progress has been made. Additionally, a protocol will need to exist for Information Transfer where experimenters and learners can share their knowledge, encourage each other, and hopefully spark insight and innovation.

Intuitive Learning Process

Instituting training and tools in a defined structure is significantly easier than attaining and retaining intuitive knowledge workers in an organization.

The amazing technology we hold in our hands, the ability to travel around the globe in hours instead of weeks, the medical tools to determine our ancestry by DNA, and the incredible knowledge base of the Internet – these all were created by people who were committed to new ideas and continuous improvement. So what do these great minds have in common? They share a commitment to the following five concepts:

- **Systems Thinking** is the ability to view life as a pattern of happenings versus isolated events. Individuals with high systems thinking see how events and decisions interact and interconnect. They understand that one act, like stubbing your toe, will have repercussions on the functioning of the system, not just the toe.

- **Personal Mastery** focuses on being committed to the best an individual can be within their natural capabilities. Individuals with high personal mastery love learning and strive to be the best person they can be. They are realistic in what they can accomplish while committed to reaching their full potential.

- **Mindfulness** is all about mental models. Each person looks at life differently, based on their experiences, education, and effects of decisions made by themselves and others on their wellbeing. Individuals with high mindfulness realize that their mental models may not perfectly reflect realty. While they will have specific points of view, they are open to hear others. A level of self-awareness and self-reflection are required to increase mindfulness.

- **Shared Visions** requires having a vision and a willingness to share that vision with others. Envisioning the future opportunities, seeing potential, and being able to articulate that vision is only half of the Shared Visions battle. To be successful, an individual must also have the confidence and competence to effectively communicate that vision in a way that will connect with others and become shared. As such, building employee RelateAbility provides the foundation to more effectively build and maintain relationships by understanding Communication Styles and Core Convictions of those we work with.

- **Team Learning** does not occur because you have called a group of people a *team*. Often, we substitute the title for the discipline needed to foster a culture of continuous improvement. Team learning is about the process of developing TeamAbility – being interdependent, contributing to a shared vision/goal, working together to attain it, and the ability to create new learning from each team experience. True team learning creates high levels of trust and accountability within the team and contributes to a culture of continuous improvement.

The above concepts were originally resulted from Dr. Senge's research in 1990 on Learning Organizations. As we dig deeper into understanding organizational culture, we realize that the individual employees are the *heart* of any culture initiative, including creating a Learning Organization and culture of continuous improvement. As such, what we seek in the culture, we must also seek in the individuals they employ.

Building a culture of continuous improvement and/or becoming a Learning Organization is not a *Quarterly Initiative* that has chosen start and completion dates. Making this choice is an act of Culture Change and one that will take years to fully integrate into an organization.

Calling yourself a *Learning Organization* as part of marketing or hiring communication may benefit in the short term - but customers and employees that are truly aligned with the principles of continuous learning and innovation will become frustrated and, quite simply, leave.

Your employees will notice if your organization is not actively discussing Organizational Culture at the top and making purposeful decisions that support your stated vision, mission, and values. And they will respond accordingly.

AdaptAbility and the Multi-Generational Workplace

A lot has been written about generational differences, especially as they impact the workplace. Often, I am asked about how generations differ from each other when talking about RelateAbility and AdaptAbility.

In an effort to make sure I am writing from a place of research, I contacted Dr. David Wilkinson, Oxford University Professor and Editor of the well-known and well-respected Oxford Review in London, England. Much of the remainder of this chapter comes from the Oxford Review, and permission was provided by Dr. Wilkerson to include this vital research information in this edition of AdaptAbility.

We hear a lot about the various generations at work and their attributes: Traditionalists, Boomers, Gen X, Millennials, and now, Gen 2020. The question still remains:

Is there really any compelling evidence to suggest that generations are really different from each other?

Research Review

Recently, there has been growing skepticism around the reliability and validity of generational research as it relates to the workplace, work values, and leadership.

In 2011, Parry and Urwin reviewed the theory and evidence provided in over a decade of writing about generational differences in work values. Their findings were published in the International Journal of Management.

In 2014, Lyons and Kuron published work in the Journal of Organizational Behavior on the generational differences in the workplace as part of review of the empirical research that has been conducted up to that time.

In 2017, Rudolph, Rauvola, and Zacher published their critical review of the research on generations in the workplace, specifically around the areas of leadership. Their findings were published in "The Leadership Quarterly".

A new study by a group of researchers from America and Germany looked at the research evidence over the years to see if there is any evidence for generational differences that are relevant to leadership, followership, leadership development, and general work outcomes.

The Results

The original idea about generational differences first really raised its head in the research literature around 1927 when researchers claimed that new 'birth cohorts' bring a new set of perspectives and a form of shared consciousness to the problems that they see and face as they mature.

However, more recently a range of studies including systematic reviews and critical reviews have refuted these assertions. Additionally, they found that any difference in generational experience does not have a significant or perceptible impact on work outcomes and processes. In effect, the very latest studies are finding that any generational differences *exert a null influence* on work outcomes and processes.

Part of the problem, the researchers found, was that there is no reliable way to identify and delineate a generation. The researchers found that studies that do find generational differences firstly all use different definitions for a generation and, secondly, make a series of assumptions about the similarities of their experiences.

While we can see also differences in the 2018 understanding of leadership and work values than those held in 1950, these differences are largely a cumulative social difference. As society changes we all change and, therefore, measuring one generation against another, as society matures or changes, invalidates the vast majority of the studies.

The researchers also discovered that researchers have been guilty of reducing the complexity of social experiences to a series of easy boxes or categories called *generations*. Once a group of people are labeled, they will identify with this label and confirmation bias starts to take hold, further invalidating the research findings. For example, by asking a worker what generation they are aligned with, their answer of "Boomer" or Gen X" shows they already have a bias in their viewpoints and experiences.

> **The review of research found that there is NO reliable research evidence of generational differences in work values, which would be needed to underpin assertions about differences in work behavior between generations.**

A 2014 study found that any evidence for generational differences in the research is primarily descriptive rather than research that really identifies any factorial differences. Further, that the studies finding differences are *fractured, contradictory and fraught with methodological inconsistencies* to be able to make any claims about the existence of generational differences.

One of the 2017 studies sought to identify all of the relevant literature about leadership and generational research. In doing so, they looked at a wide range of peer-reviewed research and found that there are four primary problems with using renationalized thinking:

1. Just thinking in terms of generations creates divisions between sections of society that there is no empirical research to support.

2. Researchers focus on group differences, rather than individual differences and, when you look at any two groups for long enough, you will find differences. The issue here is that most of the previous research has been exclusive rather than inclusive.

3. The idea of generation differences is a crude model and a gross over simplification of society. There are multiple levels and differences between cultures and subcultures that frequently account for

many of the differences noted in the studies.

4. The idea of generational differences is rather deterministic, in that it suggests that one's approach and thinking will almost entirely be the result of the era one grew up in. It does not allow for any flexibility or independence of thought or perspective. Just because you grew up in the late 1990's does not determine if you are assertive, opinionated, and believe you are always right. Being a young adult, regardless of the year you were born, has more determining factor in these types of behaviors (we have all been 19 and a large majority of us thought we knew everything and refused to listen to others).

In fact, another systematic review in 2017 entitled "Myths and misconceptions about leading generations: setting the record straight" also found that there was little valid evidence of generational differences in the workplace.

In final findings, the studies argue that generational research should have been focusing on the process of social maturity as a continual process, as opposed to something only existing in one of those generations.

Existing Evidence

Although there seems to be little empirical evidence of differences of generations related to the workplace, there is some evidence that needs to be discussed.

There is strong evidence to suggest that the experience of children today is not the same as the experience of children 20 or 30 years ago. Of course, there are differences – our current workforce has email, and Google, and smartphones. The workplace 30 years ago didn't. However, to assume that these experiences transfer to significantly different sets of values and thinking from the rest of society because of your birth year has little or no valid research evidence.

There is also evidence to support the finding that younger leaders tend to be favored in times of change and difficulty and that older leaders tend to be preferred in times of stability. This has been the case since the industrial revolution, and is not specific to a generation, but rather a larger human behavior when dealing with change and the realities of the human development lifecycle.

Researchers did find that a lifespan developmental approach provides a much better way of looking at age, work outcomes and leadership. From this perspective, learning and development is seen as a lifelong process for every individual, regardless of when they were born. The important difference here is that any generational differences are seen to emanate from experience and knowledge. It stands to reason that the older, more established employees are likely to know more and have more experience to draw on.

Therefore, taking each individual as a *work in progress* and helping them to develop, learn, share knowledge, and seek further understanding is a much more useful perspective than reducing and stereotyping people into a generational label.

Life Span Development

The latest research focused on generational and leadership differences shows that there is no real valid empirical evidence for a generational divide in terms of work outcomes and leadership.

The idea of the lifespan development approach has received a lot of research support over the last 30 years and treats people as individuals, while stopping over-generalization and stereotyping.

Understanding life span differences and building relationships between older and younger workers are critical to improving organizational and employee performance.

When all is said and done, people are people. Regardless of the year of our birth or our generational label, we all experience change via the Change Curve and we all have the opportunity to build our RelateAbility and AdaptAbility to make our work and lives better.

As situations in our lives change, we will find ourselves in a state of heightened emotions. We will want to desperately hold onto what we know in the **NOW**. Many would agree that we don't make our best decisions when we are emotional. Some of our worst decisions are the result of not taking the time to pause, to mind the gap between **NOW** and **NEXT**, between Discomfort and Discovery. Choosing to pause, reflect, and reframe at the critical transition point gives us the space needed to make more effective and educated choices.

Make a Plan

If we have the map ahead of time, we can make a much better plan. The Change Curve is a map that we can effectively use to prioritize, plan for, and be better prepared for changes when they occur. Leveraging our Curiosity to identify our place on the Change Curve will help us understand how we are thinking, feeling, and behaving because of the shift in situation or circumstance. Identifying where others are on the Change Curve will help us better support and empower them to move forward and not get stuck in the *Wallow Waltz.*

Remembering the six D's of Change will create a map that will equip, empower, enable, and engage you in the process of change. By having the plan, you are no longer required to *just survive* but rather choose to *thrive* during times of uncertainty.

If you know a change is coming, I encourage you to work through the success strategies and identify support actions that you can have in place to decrease your performance gap and accelerate your journey through to Discovery.

Reason Well

People often jump to conclusions. Sometimes our conclusions are accurate, and sometimes they can be *way out in left field*. Our conclusions, when expressed to others, have influence. Our points of view will impact how others make their choices. As we seek to improve our AdaptAbility, it is important to be aware of how we come to our conclusions, and adjust our behaviors.

One of my favorite models describes the thinking process we go through, usually without realizing it, to transition from receiving data or facts to a decision or action. In 1970, Dr. Chris Argyris of Harvard University conducted research and created a visual model to help us better understand this subconscious process of decision making. He called it the Ladder of Inference. This tool became widely known when Dr. Senge referenced it in his work about organizational learning and continuous improvement.

Below is the Ladder of Influence with each rung representing a step in our decision-making process. Like a ladder, we will begin at the bottom and move upwards.

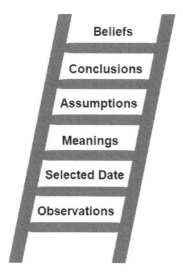

Starting at the bottom of the ladder, we have reality and facts that enter our brains as **observations**. From there, we experience these data sets **selectively** based on our beliefs and prior experience. Once we have data selected, we prioritize and attempt to interpret what they **mean**. Next, we overlay our existing **assumptions**, sometimes without considering them, to the meaning we have drawn from the select data we have chosen. With this new set of meaning we draw **conclusions** based on the interpreted facts and our own assumptions and values. From here, we create **beliefs**, like what is correct or incorrect, based on these conclusions. Finally, we take **actions** that seem *right* because they are based on what we believe to be true. In many cases, this all happens in a fraction of a second.

Do you see the potential for error in this process?

All the conclusions we create are based on prior set beliefs, which are the basis for the brain to select which data will influence our decisions. This can lead us to ignore certain facts altogether!

So how do we protect ourselves from action based on selective assumptions and partial data? Well, we go back to the ladder and choose to take a few steps back in our reasoning process.

By being aware of the Ladder of Inference, we can review the rationality of our decisions. We can choose to get back to the facts and use our beliefs and experiences consciously and make better and more effective decisions. By being more aware of how we make quick decisions and choosing to pull deep on our strength of curiosity and wonder – we can catch ourselves making assumptions and beliefs that could cause conflict or errors to occur.

This is a very turbulent time in our history. It seems everyone is screaming their own opinion about what is and what isn't. No one seems to be listening to each other, and even fewer are choosing to take a step back and entertain the strength of curiosity and wonder.

Do we quickly press the share button or retweet the view of someone we may not even know is credible or reliable?

What if we were to take a moment to verify that the statements we are reposting online were actually true?

Are we willing to do the extra work to validate the facts and messages that so quickly resonate with our personal beliefs?

Finally, I want to encourage us to seek information, data, and perspectives that may be different than our own. Just because we listen to them, does not require us to believe them. The alternative is believing only what we think is right, without facts or data to support our views and statements.

Critically thinking is a personal choice and responsibility. Instead of acting out in assumption, let us choose to exercise maturity and share viewpoints that have been reasoned well, showing respect and dignity to all involved.

Take the LEAD

One of my favorite sayings is:

Education without Application is just Useless Information!

Having Awareness without it impacting Behavior, runs the same result – a good read, but no real change. Taking the **LEAD** isn't about taking control or power in a shifting situation or circumstance. Taking the LEAD reflects the following:

- **Learn** – Challenge yourself to be a life-long learner. Immerse yourself in new ideas and insights, especially those that are different than your own. For me, I absolutely love listening to TedTalks on TED.com, sometimes I just randomly select one to learn something new or gain a new insight on how others see our world.

- **Engage** – Challenge yourself to connect with others and participate in change initiatives. We are all hardwired for connection. Understanding ourselves is powerful, but connecting and engaging in great conversation and learning about others brings a whole new level to living your best life. Proactively seeking ways to make a difference, no matter how small, is still choosing to engage in the life you are living.

- **Appreciate** – Challenge yourself to seek opportunities to communicate your appreciation to others for their behaviors and choices. There is a proverb that says, "What You Seek, You Will Find". Choose to seek the good in others, the beauty in a moment, the benefit of the change, or simply be grateful for the breath you breathe.

- **Deliver** – Challenge yourself to be accountable, to do what you say you will do. So many great ideas and efforts fail because we don't deliver on what we have promised. I love the saying by Dr. Arnold Beckman "There is no substitute for excellence." Make it habit to under promise and over deliver as we seek excellence in all we choose to do.

Learning, Engaging, Appreciating, and Delivering are hallmarks of a great leader. They are also hallmarks of a great Change Champion. Leadership is about influence, not position. Everyone has the ability to positively influence the behaviors of others. In, fact, that is the definition of Leadership!

Regardless of where you are, you have opportunities to **LEAD**, you only have to choose to do so.

Closing Thoughts

As you explored the chapters of this book, I hope you took the time to ask yourself the following questions:

Who am I being?

How does this information impact me in the real world?

How can I apply what I am reading to the personal and organizational shifts I am experiencing?

Equip yourself, engage others, empower discovery - and when shift happens - you can rise and shine, take up the challenge, and...

Choose AdaptAbility!

Research and Resources

Ackerman, L. (1982). *Transition Management: An In-depth Look at Managing Complex Change.* Organizational Dynamics, 42-66.

Adams, J.D. & Spencer, S.A. (1988). "People in Transition." Training and Development Journal. Oct. p.61-63.

Aguirre, D., vonPost, R., and Alpern, M. (2013). Culture's Role in Enabling Organizational Change. Booz & Company.

Argyris, C. (1982). "The executive mind and double-loop learning." Organizational Dynamics, 11(2), 5-22.

Argyris, C. (1990) *Overcoming Organizational Defenses. Facilitating Organizational Learning,* 1st Edition.

Badham, R., Mead, A. and Antonacopoulou, A. (2012) "Performing change: A dramaturgical approach to the practice of managing change." In: Boje DM, Burnes B and Hassard J (eds) Routledge Companion to Organizational Change. London: Routledge, 187–205.

Baron, R.A. (1983) *Behavior in Organizations: Understanding and Managing the Human Side of Work.* Boston, MA: Allyn & Bacon.

Barrett, F. J. (1995). *Creating Appreciative Learning Cultures.* Organizational Dynamics, 24(1), 36-49.

Becher, T. and Trowler, P. (2001) *Academic Tribes and Territories*, 2nd edn. Maidenhead: The Society for Research into Higher Education and Open University Press.

Beck, R.N. (1987) "Visions, Values, and Strategies: Changing attitudes and culture." The Academy of Management Executive 1(1): 33–41.

Beer, M. (1987) *Revitalizing organizations: Change process and emergent model*. The Academy of Management Executive 1(1): 51–55.

Bell, S.T.(2007). "Deep-level Composition Variables as Predictors of Team Performance: A Meta-analysis." Journal of Applied Psychology, 92(3): 595-615.

Blom, T. and Viljoen, R. *Human Reactions To Change*.

Booz & Company. (2004) *An Overall Approach to Change Management*.

Bridges, W. (1994). *Job Shift*. Addison-Wesley.

Bridges, W. (1990). *Surviving Corporate Transition*. William Bridges & Associates.

Bridges, W. (1980). *Transitions: Making Sense of Life's Changes*. Addison-Wesley.

Bridges, W. (1991). *Managing Transition: Making the Most of Change*. Addison-Wesley.

Brock, L.R, and Solerno, A. (1994) *The Change Cycle: The Secret to Getting Through Life's Difficult Changes*. Bridge Builder Media.

Burke, W.W. (1982) *Organization Development: Principles and Practices*. Boston, MA: Little Brown.

Burnes, B. (2004a) "Kurt Lewin and the planned approach to change: A re-appraisal." Journal of Management Studies 41(6): 977–1002.

Burnes, B. (2004b) "Kurt Lewin and complexity theories: Back to the future?" Journal of Change Management 4(4): 309–325.

Burnes, B. (2007) "Kurt Lewin and the Harwood Studies: The foundations of OD." The Journal of Applied Behavioral Science 43(2): 213–231.

Burnes, B. (2009) *Managing Change*. London: Prentice Hall.

Clark, L., et al. (2004). "The neuropsychology of ventral prefrontal cortex: decision-making and reversal learning." Brain and Cognition 55(1): 41-53.

Conner, D. (1993). *Managing at the Speed of Change*, New York, Villard.

Cooperrider, D. L. (1986). "Appreciative Inquiry: Toward a Methodology for Understanding and Enhancing Organizational Innovation." Unpublished Doctoral Dissertation, Case Western Reserve University, Cleveland, Ohio.

Cooperrider, D. L. (1990). *Positive Image, Positive Action: The Affirmative Basis of Organizing*. In S. Srivastva & D. L. Cooperrider (Eds.), Appreciative Management and Leadership: The Power of Positive Thought and Action in Organizations . San Francisco, CA: Jossey-Bass.

Cooperrider, D. L., & Pasmore, W. A. (1991). *The Organization Dimension of Global Change*. Human Relations, 44(8), 763-787.

Corporate Executive Board. (2007) *Change Management Model of Roles and Responsibilities*. CEB Global.

Corporate Executive Board. (2007) *Process and Tactics for Communicating Change: A Three-Pronged Approach to Managing Change during Difficult Business Climates*. CEB Global.

Corporate Executive Board. (2008) *Managing Corporate Cultural Change*. CEB Global.

Corporate Executive Board. (2008) *Manager's Toolkit for Managing Change*. CEB Global.

Corporate Executive Board (2008). *Change Management Fundamentals – An Introduction to Managing Change*. CEB Global.

Corporate Executive Board (2016). *Executive Guidance: Boosting Corporate Performance During Change Initiatives*. CEB Global.

Corporate Leadership Council. (2008) *Manager's Checklist for Communicating Change*. CEB Global.

Corporate Leadership Council. (2009) *Building Employee Commitment to Change*. CEB Global.

Collins, D. (1998) *Organizational Change: Sociological Perspectives*. Routledge: London.

Cummings TG and Worley CG (2009) *Organizational Development and Change*, 9th edn. Cincinnati, OH: SouthWestern.

DeChurch, L.A., & Mesmer-Magnus, J.R.(2010). "The Cognitive Underpinnings of Effective Teamwork: A Meta-analysis." Journal of Applied Psychology, 95(1): 32-53.

Deloitte University Press.(2017). "2017 Global Human Capital Trends." https://bit.ly/2gNr304.

Deloitte University Press.(2016). "2016 Global Human Capital Trends." https://bit.ly/2NNoOJl.

Demers, R., Forrer, S.E., Leibowitz, Z., Cahill, C. (1996). "Commitment to Change." Training and Development Journal. Aug. p.22-26.

Dent, EN and Goldberg, SG (1999) "Challenging 'resistance to change." The Journal of Applied Behavioral Science 35(1): 25–41.

Duhigg, C.(2016). "What Google Learned from its Quest to Build the Perfect Team." The New York Times Magazine. https://nyti.ms/2nn3Bg4.

Elrod, P. D., & Tippett, D. D. (1999). "An empirical study of the relationship between team performance and team maturity." Engineering Management Journal 11(1): 7-14.

Elrod, P. D. and D. D. Tippett (2002). "The "death valley" of change." Journal of Organizational Change Management 15(3): 273-291.

French, W.L. and Bell, C.H. (1995) *Organization Development,* 5th edn. Englewood Cliffs, NJ: Prentice-Hall.

French, W.L., Bell, C.H. and Zawacki, R.A. (2005) *Organization Development and Transformation.* New York: McGraw Hill.

Galpin, T. (1996). "Connecting Culture to Organizational Change." Human Resource Management. Mar. p.84-90.

Gentry, B. (2014). *Coaching People Through The Change Curve.* The Insights Group Ltd.

Haas, M. & Mortenson, M. (2016). "The Secrets of Great Teamwork." Harvard Business Review. https://bit.ly/1YCeItP.

Hamlin, B. (2016). "HRD and Organizational Change: Evidence-Based Practice." International Journal of HRD Policy, Practice, and Research. Volume 1: 7-20.

Harlow, H. F. (1949). "The formation of learning sets." Psychological Review 56(1): 51.

Harman, W. W. (1990). *Shifting Context for Executive Behavior: Signs of Change and Revaluation.* In S. Srivastva, D. L. Cooperrider, & Associates (Eds.), Appreciative Management and Leadership: The Power of Positive Thought and Action in Organizations (1st ed., pp. 37-54). San Francisco, CA: Jossey-Bass Inc.

Hendry, C. (1996) "Understanding and creating whole organizational change through learning theory." Human Relations 49(5): 621–641.

Jeffcutt, P. (1996) "Between managers and the managed: The processes of organizational transition." In: Linstead S, Small RG and Jeffcutt, P. (eds) Understanding Management. London: SAGE, 172–193.

Kaltenecker, S. and K. Leopold (2015). *Kanban Change Leadership: Creating a Culture of Continuous Improvement* 1st Edition, Wiley.

Kanter, R.M., Stein, B. and Jick, T. (1992) *The Challenge of Organizational Change.* New York: The Free Press.

Kaplan, R.S., & Norton, D.P. (1996) "Strategic Planning and the Balanced Scorecard." Strategy & Leadership, Vol. 24, No. 5, pp. 18-24.

Kelman, H.C. (1958) "Compliance, identification, and internalization: Three processes of attitude change." The Journal of Conflict Resolution 2(1): 51–60.

Kotter, J.P. (1995) "Leading change: Why transformation efforts fail." Harvard Business Review 73(2): 59–67.

Kotter, J.P. and Cohen, D.S. (2002) *The Heart of Change: Real-life Stories of How People Change their Organizations.* Boston, MA: Harvard Business Press.

Kotter, J.P., and Rathgeber, H. (2006) *Our Iceberg is Melting: Changing and Succeeding Under Any Conditions.* London: Macmillan.

Kozlowski, S.W.J.& Bell, B.F.(2001).*Work Groups and Teams in Organizations.* https://bit.ly/2hJARHd.

Kubler-Ross, E. and Byock, I. (2014). *On Death and Dying.* Scribner.

Kubler-Ross, E., Kessler, D. and Shriver, M. (2014) *On Grief and Grieving.* Scribner.

Langley, A., Smallman, C., Tsoukas, H. and Van de Ven, A.H. (2009) "Process studies of change in organization and management." Academy of Management Journal 52(3): 629–630.

Lencioni, Patrick M.(2002).*The Five Dysfunctions of a Team: A Leadership Fable.* Jossey-Bass.

Lewin, K. (1951). *Field theory in social science.* New York: Harper and Row.

Lewis, S., Passmore, J. & Cantore, S. (2007). *Appreciative inquiry for change management: Using AI to facilitate organizational development.* London: Kogan Page.

Lippitt, R., Watson, J., Westley, B. and Spalding, W.B. (1958) *The Dynamics of Planned Change: A Comparative Study of Principles and Techniques.* New York: Harcourt Brace.

Losada, M. & Heaphy, E. (2004). "The role of positivity and connectivity in the performance of business teams." American Behavioral Scientist, 47(6), 740–765.

Ludema, J., Wilmot, T., & Srivastva, S. (1997). "Organizational Hope: Reaffirming the Constructive Task of Social and Organizational Inquiry." Human Relations, 50(8), 1015-1052.

Lyons, S., & Kuron, L. (2014). "Generational differences in the workplace: A review of the evidence and directions for future research." Journal of Organizational Behavior, 35(S1).

Mantere, S., Schildt, H.A., and Sillince, J.A. (2012) "Reversal of strategic change." Academy of Management Journal 55(1): 172–196.

Maslow, A.H. (1954). *Motivation and Personality* (3rd edn). New York: Harper and Row.

McGregor, D. (1960). *The Human Side of Enterprise*. New York: McGraw-Hill.

McKenna, E. (2012) *Business Psychology and Organizational Behaviour*. Psychology Press.

McKenna, E. (2013) *Human Resource Management*, 3rd Edition. Trans-Atlantic Publications, Inc.

Miner, J. (2005). *Organizational behavior: Essential theories of motivation and leadership*. New York: M.E. Sharpe.

Nadler, D.A. and Tushman, M.L. (1989) "Organizational frame bending: Principles for managing reorientation." Academy of Management Executive 3(3): 194–204.

Nikula, U., et al. (2010). "Empirical validation of the Classic Change Curve on a software technology change project." Information and Software Technology 52(6): 680-696.

O'Neil, M. (2000) *Executive Coaching: with Backbone and Heart*, San Francisco, Jossey-Bass Publishers.

Palmer, I. and Dunford, R. (2008) "Organizational change and the importance of embedded assumptions." British Journal of Management 19(1): 20–32.

Palmer, I., Dunford, R. and Akin, G. (2009) *Managing Organizational Change: A Multiple Perspectives Approach.* New York: McGraw-Hill Irwin.

Parry, E., & Urwin, P. (2011). "Generational differences in work values: A review of theory and evidence." International journal of management reviews, 13(1), 79-96.

Price Waterhouse. *Change Integration Team (1995) Better Change: Best Practices for Transforming Your Organization.* New York: Irwin Professional Publishing.

Pritchett, Price & Pound, Ron. *A Survival Guide to the Stress of Organizational Change.*

Pritchett, Price. (1987), *The Employee Survival Guide to Mergers & Acquisitions.*

Pritchett, Price & Pound, Ron. (1990). *The Employee Handbook for Organizational Change.*

Pritchett, Price & Pound, Ron. (1992). *Building a High Performance Work Group During Change.*

Pritchett, Price. (1996). *Resistance, Moving Beyond the Barriers to Change.*

Rainey, M. A. (1996). "An Appreciative Inquiry Into the Factors of Culture Continuity During Leadership Transition."

Organization Development Practitioner, 28(1&2), 34-41. contact: 201-763-7337.

Rafferty, A. and Restubog, S. (2016) *Why do employees perception of an organisational's change history matter?* Human Resource Management.

Renn, R. W., Steinbauer, R., & Biggane, J. (2018). "Reconceptualizing self-defeating work behavior for management research." Human Resource Management Review, 28(2), 131-143.

Rheem, H. (1995). "The Learning Organization." Harvard Business Review. Vol. 73, No. 2, p. 10.

Robbins, S. and Judge, T.A. (2009) *Organizational Behavior: Concepts, Controversies, and Applications*, 13th edn. Upper Saddle River, NJ: Prentice-Hall.

Royal, C. (1994) *The NTL Diversity Study, The Use of Appreciative Inquiry to Discover Best Experiences Around Diversity in a Professional OD Organization.* NTL Institute for Applied Behavioral Science, Alexandra, VA.

Rudolph, C. W., Rauvola, R. S., & Zacher, H. (2017). "Leadership and generations at work: a critical review." The Leadership Quarterly.

Rudolph, C. W. & Zacher, H. (2017). "Myths and misconceptions about leading generations:Setting the record straight." In T. A. Scandura & E. Mourino (Eds.), Leading diversity in the 21st century (pp. 243–278). Charlotte, NC: Information Age Publishing.

Sandholtz, W. and Stiles, K. (2008) *International Norms and Cycles of Change* 1st Edition. Oxford University Press.

Salerno, A. and Brock, LR. (2008). *The Change Cycle: How People Can Survive and Thrive in Organizational Change.* Berret-Koehler Publishers.

Schein, E.H. (1985) *Organizational Culture and Leadership.* San Francisco, CA: Jossey-Bass.

Schein, E.H. (1988) *Organizational Psychology,* 3rd edn. London: Prentice-Hall.

Schein, E.H. (1992) *Organizational Culture and Leadership,* 2nd edn. San Francisco, CA: Jossey-Bass.

Schein, E.H. (1996) "Kurt Lewin's change theory in the field and in the classroom: Notes toward a model of managed learning." Systems Practice 9(1): 27–47.

Schein, E.H. (2010) *Organizational Culture and Leadership,* 4th edn. San Francisco, CA: Wiley.

Schein, E.H. and Bennis WG (1965) *Personal and Organizational Change Through Group Methods: The Laboratory Approach.* New York: Wiley.

Scott, C.D. & Jaffe, D.T. (1991). "From Crisis to Culture Change." Health Care Forum Journal. May/June p.33-41.

Scott, C.D. & Jaffe, D.T. (1993). *Stress & Stress Management in the Workplace.* In M.P. O'Donnell, J.S. Harris (eds), Health Promotion in the Workplace. Delmar.

Senge, P. M. (1996). "Leading Learning Organizations." Training & Development, Vol. 50, No. 12, pp. 36-4.

Senge, P. M. (2014). *The fifth discipline fieldbook: Strategies and tools for building a learning organization.* Crown Business.

Sonenshein, S. (2010) "We're changing – or are we? Untangling the role of progressive, regressive, and stability narratives during strategic change implementation." Academy of Management Journal 53(3): 477–512.

Stacey, R.D. (2007) *Strategic Management and Organisational Dynamics: The Challenge of Complexity,* 5th edn. Harlow: Prentice Hall.

Stanley et al. (2015). *Team of Teams: New Rules of Engagement for a Complex World.* Penguin Publishing Group.

Thachenkery, T. J. (1996). "Affirmation as Facilitation: A Postmodernist Paradigm in Change Management." Organization Development Practitioner, 28(1), 12-22.

Tompkins, T. C. & Rhodes, K. (2012). "Groupthink and the ladder of inference: Increasing effective decision making." The Journal of Human Resource and Adult Learning, 8(2), 84.

Tsoukas, H. and Chia, R. (2002) "On organizational becoming: Rethinking organizational change." Organization Science 13(5): 567–582.

Tsoukas, H. and Cummings, S. (1997) "Marginalization and recovery: The emergence of Aristotelian themes in organization studies." Organization Studies 18(4): 655–683.

Tuckman, Bruce W (1965). "Developmental Sequence in Small Groups." Psychological Bulletin, 63(6): 384–399.

Tuckman, B. & Jensen, M. (1977). "Stages of small-group development revisited." Group and Organization Studies. December 1977, 2(4), 419-427.

Tushman, M. (1974) "Organizational Change: An Exploratory Study and Case History." Ithaca, NY:ILR Press, Cornell University.

Waddell, D. (2007) *Contemporary Management*. North Ryde, NSW: McGraw-Hill Irwin.

Waddell, D.M., Creed, A., Cummings, T.G. and Worley, C.G. (2014) *Organizational Change: Development and Transformation*, 5th edn. Melbourne: Cengage.

Weick, K.E. and Quinn, R.E. (1999) "Organizational change and development." Annual Review of Psychology 50(1): 361–386.

Worren, N.A., Ruddle, K., and Moore, K. (1999) "From organizational development to change management: The emergence of a new profession." The Journal of Applied Behavioral Science 35(3): 273–286.

Watkins, J. M., & Cooperrider, D. L. (1996). "Organizational Inquiry Model For Global Social Change Organizations." Organization Development Journal, 14(4), 97-112.

Wilkinson, D.J. & Manning, T (2018). "Defining Self-Defeating Work Behaviors. Research Briefing." The Oxford Review. www.oxford-review.com.